Trish Deseine

celebrating with friends

photography by Marie-Pierre Morel

contents

Digest this first!

Let's make one thing clear: this book is not for diplomats or do-it-yourself (DIY) buffs.

Diplomats give sparkling soirées, arranged entirely by telephone. Such gatherings feature ice sculptures, pyramids of champagne, designer canapés, and caterers who whip up delicious little dishes on the spot, all the while discreetly filling your glass. It's marvelous. Get yourself invited.

The DIYs, on the other hand, have done it all themselves. They've poured out packets of peanuts and bags of chips onto paper plates with their own hands. They've spread 342 cold blinis with taramasalata and 433 slices of toast with pâté garnished with gherkins. They've heated cans of cocktail sausages at the beginning of the evening, then left them cooling on the sideboard next to the dry mustard and the delicious dessert brought by guests.

You've guessed it. At-home gatherings cannot be half-baked affairs. Not to be confused with the last-minute casual meals thrown together to fit in with life's everyday pressures, a party should be anticipated, planned, thought-through, prepared – or it's not a party.

The ten rules of a well-planned party

Relax. The effort required has more to do with brainpower than brawn. Forget sophistication and difficulty. Go for simplicity and, as best as possible, for quality ingredients. Follow these ten rules (I've left out some obvious ones like warning the neighbors, setting aside a spot for the coats, making coffee in presentable vacuum flasks, etc.,). Let yourself be inspired by the recipes and themes of this book and all will go well.

1 You are neither Alice Waters nor Jacques Pepin.

This time, you are not going to use caterers. So whatever you do, don't copy their presentations. This applies for dinners and lunches: do not try to re-create professional catering. If you want to try a chef's cooking, go to their restaurant. If you want magnificent and identical appetizers, buy them to-go.

Get some ideas from the professionals – then do it your way – simply but with imagination, using the best ingredients you can afford.

As for the drinks, try to coordinate the alcohol. A decent wine you have discovered and bought in quantity will go down better throughout the evening than an assortment from guests. This will avoid hangovers and the spoiling of good wines being served at either the wrong temperature or at the wrong moment or both.

2 Think like an interior designer.

Remember the best parties when you were young? Glasses constantly refilled and music in the background. Guests squashed like sardines in half-darkness, forced to make conversation, obliged to dance, incapable of not amusing themselves.

If you want a sparkling ambiance, don't let your guests disperse, and do not put the dance floor in a remote corner of the house. In any case, around midnight everyone will gather in the kitchen. So think carefully where to locate the buffet. Nothing dampens the atmosphere more than guests waiting their turn in a line reminiscent of a school cafeteria. If you have more than 25, it's better to plan for two buffet tables with identical dishes, china, cutlery, glasses, and decoration.

3 China, cutlery, glasses: make sure you have plenty or hire them.

Kitchenware shops are overflowing with white china. You can get plates at very reasonable prices. Go for medium plates and shallow bowls that can be used for salad, dessert, or soup.

When I have more than 40 guests, I rent china and glasses. White or plain ones cost less. Moreover, you can put them back into their boxes immediately after they've been used, hidden under the buffet tablecloth. Not having to do the washing up is the height of decadence. You just return them!

4 If you have 25 guests or more, get help.

Essential, if you want to enjoy your own party. I've often turned my babysitters into impeccable waitresses, thanks to an apron and a good briefing. Compared with tending my four wild kids, dealing with 60 lit-up guests is a piece of cake.

5 Don't improvise the music.

Overheated audio systems, amateur DJ dictators with a passion for Fleetwood Mac – it is VERY difficult to please everyone and to equip yourself appropriately.

It's easy to keep 20 good friends grooving for an hour or two with simple CDs of everyone's favorites and a good auto-changer, so that you don't find yourself exhausted by the end of the evening.

But if it's a party where the generations are mixed (a wedding or engagement party) and you want all-night dancing for 50 guests, it is essential to find a good DJ from a good club or from another party.

It's a skill. DJs know how to read the mood at every moment and to adjust their play list. They have great material and love hosting all types of parties.

6 For children? There's always a solution!

Ten year-olds and under

If you plan a party for this age group, have babysitters to watch the little ones, a suitable menu, and a place where they can rest, watch a video, or sleep later on.

But having young children at a party for adults is strongly discouraged. I've tried it. Imagine a 12-month-old baby passed among the guests like a plate of sandwiches until 9:30. There's nothing like it to ruin the mood, make stains, and translate your femme fatale image into that of a mother hen.

Other examples: thanks to big brothers, we twice came within a hair's breath of fire. The first time it was through cocoa spilled over Hubert's tape deck and portable (sorry, Huby), and the second time it was caused by obsessive relighting of the adorable candles set at floor level.

If your children are like mine, once they're asleep, not even Dancing Queen bawled in a hundred-decibel chorus by all the guests just below their room will wake them. The problem is to get them asleep BEFORE the guests arrive.

Try to distribute several of the tribe among other guests and provide a seasoned babysitter to leave them free to party themselves.

Teenagers

They can be a problem. There are two scenarios: either they make you feel like old, wrinkly has-beens by snickering in a corner, howling with laughter at the sight of your guests rocking to their Eminem CD, or you're the sort of parents who manage to override their adolescent angst and press them into service as DJs. Either way, don't oblige them to attend.

7 Groups of friends.

We all have different groups of friends. To get them talking to each other, try a themed party (avoid Barbie & Ken before May because of the need for a suntan, Ben Hur, or The Man in the Iron Mask because of the costume rental costs). Or an easy quiz premise – 'What am I?' with clues given to everyone as they arrive – could work well. But beware, some people may take it badly to find themselves classified as 'mad cow' (sorry, Sophie).

Don't worry too much about making people intermingle – they will do it of their own accord, eventually, if the ambience is right.

Older people

I don't share the ageism of certain adolescents, as mentioned in the preceding paragraph. My friends aged 60 and upwards have all of life's experience to impart, another freer life ahead of them, and nothing to prove. Those who come to my parties enjoy mixing and chatting with everyone and are the last to leave the dance floor. It's up to you.

8 Appetite comes with eating, thirst with drinking. Think about the feeding timetable.

There's always a critical moment, after the first or second glass, when the appetite of your guests revives like that of the giant in Tom Thumb.

To start with, you will have provided little hors d'oeuvres, dips, or other DIY nibbles. But when the Great Hunger strikes, serve a soup, or a substantial sandwich, then carry on with the hors d'oeuvres before bringing on a 'main' dish.

It is very important that glasses can be refilled easily. Always, make sure that guests can get to the drinks, and delegate one or two friends to make the rounds with a bottle of champagne or mineral water.

9 Calculate the quantities.

Very, very difficult. I have no tips to impart. Even when I have followed expert advice, I always make twice as much of the food that is leftover and half as much of the food that is gobbled down immediately.

Another terribly unfair point: even if the food is divine, if there isn't enough, your guests will remember only that they left feeling hungry and unsatisfied.

10 Serve food that's easy to eat.

Go for finger food or fork food. For a buffet party, avoid everything that runs, drips, disintegrates in the hand, needs knife and fork, or requires a more solid support than a pair of knees. Instead, take advantage of the wide range of breads (baguettes, ciabatta, focaccia, sourdough) to be found in the supermarket.

That vital spark

That's the end of my planning advice – now, on to the recipes.

All of this, however, is simply set decor and props for the production. The most important element is the actors: you and your guests.

You cannot manufacture atmosphere – the sparkle that will turn your party into a wonderful evening to be talked about for years. This magic is a rare and precious ingredient for which, unfortunately, I don't have the recipe.

A housewarming for paupers

We all know the feeling: we're so thrilled with our new home that we simply have to throw a party to celebrate.

But every last penny has gone toward the mortgage or down payment. How to do it well and cheaply?

Firstly, a BYO (bring your own) is required. Careful, this should not resemble the BYOB (bring your own booze) of college parties. A BYO should take the form of a bottle of champagne per head, gracefully suggested on the invitation card with a stylish addition 'bubbles appreciated' or the other 'BYOB' (bring your own bubbles).

This will reduce costs, avoid the hangovers caused by a mix of wine and assorted spirits, and ensure a real party atmosphere all evening. All the same, make sure to keep two bottles chilled to await the arrival of other guests.

The food should be very simple, seasonal, and based around bread, pasta, fruit, and vegetables. It's worth searching out good bread and going to your local market for all the other products. The more an ingredient is in season, the better and cheaper it will be. Take advantage of this.

Tomato and chili

Makes a small bowlful
Preparation time: 3 minutes

1 cup peeled canned tomatoes, drained and lightly chopped
2 tbsp olive oil
1 tsp chili sauce (optional)
Sea salt and freshly ground pepper

Mix all the ingredients and add the chili sauce, if you like
things hot!

Avocado, tomato, mascarpone, and lime

Makes a small bowlful
Preparation time: 10 minutes

1 tomato, peeled
2 avocados, peeled
2 tbsp mascarpone cheese
Juice of 2 limes
Salt and pepper

Mash the avocados and mix with the other ingredients.
Season to taste.

Feta and red bell pepper

Makes a small bowlful
Preparation time: 15 minutes

1 cup Greek feta cheese, crumbled
1 red bell pepper, diced
½ cup heavy cream
Sea salt and pepper

Mix the ingredients with a fork until they reach
a smooth consistency.

Hummus and pine nuts

Makes a small bowlful
Preparation time: 15 minutes
Cooking time: 15 minutes

1 can (15 oz) garbanzo beans, drained and rinsed
3 to 4 tbsp olive oil
8 tbsp lemon juice
2 tbsp tahini
4 to 5 tbsp pine nuts, toasted
Salt and pepper

Blend the garbanzos in a food processor with the olive oil,
lemon juice (to taste), tahini, and half the pine nuts. Season
to taste.

Serve in a bowl for dipping or spreading, decorated with the
rest of the pine nuts.

Toasted brioche, chicken liver pâté with port, and juniper berries

Serves 6
Preparation time: 10 minutes
Cooking time: 15 minutes

4 tbsp olive oil
1 shallot, chopped
1 cup chicken livers
2 tbsp port
5 juniper berries, crushed
6 slices of brioche, toasted
Italian parsley, chives (snipped), or chutney
Sea salt and pepper

Heat 2 tablespoons of olive oil in a pan. Cook the shallot gently then add the chicken livers. When they are well done on the outside, but still pink inside, deglaze the pan with the port.

Remove the livers, and process finely with the cooking liquid and the juniper berries.

Season, adding olive oil if the mixture is too dry.

Spread on the brioche slices and garnish with parsley, chives, or chutney.

Garlic bread

Serves 6
Preparation time: 5 minutes
Cooking time: 10 minutes

2/3 cup butter, softened
2 garlic cloves, crushed
1 tbsp parsley, finely chopped
Pepper
1 baguette

Blend together the garlic, parsley, and butter, and season with the pepper. Slice the baguette lengthways without cutting right through. Spread with the garlic butter, close up the baguette, and cook at 350°F for about 10 minutes or until golden.

Slice and serve.

Crostini with red onion jam and goat cheese

Serves 6 to 8
Preparation time: 10 minutes
Cooking time: 1 hour

1/3 cup raisins
Olive oil
1 lb red onions, finely sliced
1/3 cup sugar
2/3 cup red wine
2 tbsp balsamic vinegar
1 tbsp crème de cassis
2 thin sticks French bread (ficelles or 2 thin loafs about half the size of a baguette)
3 small packages of fresh goat cheese

Steep the raisins in hot water for around 30 minutes. Drain and set aside.

Heat 2 to 3 tablespoons of oil in a pan. Cook the onions over a low heat for 10 to 15 minutes or until golden.

Add the sugar, lower the heat, and continue cooking for 10 minutes, until the onions are well softened and caramelized.

Add the raisins, wine, vinegar, and crème de cassis, and cook for 25 to 30 minutes until all the liquid is absorbed. Season and let cool.

Heat the oven to 350°F.

Slice the bread in rounds and put on an ovenproof plate, adding a few drops of oil to each slice.

Bake for 4 to 5 minutes. Cool before spreading with the onion jam. Top each slice with a nugget of goat cheese.

Almond croutons

Makes 48 croutons
Preparation time: 15 minutes
Cooking time: 5 minutes

1/3 cup chopped almonds
1 tsp sea salt
12 slices white sandwich bread, crusts removed
2/3 cup butter, melted

Preheat the oven to 400°F.

Mix together the almonds and salt. Dip each side of the bread in melted butter then into the almonds. Put on greaseproof paper or a silicone mat in an ovenproof dish, and bake until golden, about 5 minutes.

Remove from the oven and let cool on a rack.

Angel hair frittata with bacon and cheese

Makes 25 pieces
Preparation time: 15 minutes
Cooking time: 5 minutes

7 oz bacon, cut into strips
6 eggs
4 tbsp crème fraîche
2 tbsp chives, chopped
½ cup Parmesan, grated
½ lb angel hair pasta, cooked according to package instructions
Butter, for frying

Lightly brown the bacon in a frying pan, let drain on paper towels, and set aside.

Beat the eggs with the crème fraîche and season lightly. Add the chives, Parmesan, and bacon, and stir into the pasta. Melt the butter in a pan and pour in the mixture. Cook very gently until the eggs begin to set and the top is golden. Turn and cook the underside. Remove from the pan and slice into wedges.

Serve warm or cold.

Note. To help turn the frittata, first slide it onto a plate and cover with another plate. Turn over and slide the frittata back into the pan.

Tartlets with tongue, capers, and croutons

Serves: 6
Preparation time: 10 minutes
Cooking time: 5 minutes for the croutons

½ baguette
1 garlic clove, peeled
Olive oil
2 to 3 slices beef tongue, from the deli counter
2 tbsp capers
1 tbsp parsley, chopped
6 small pastry shells
Salt and pepper

Preheat the oven to 350°F.

To make the croutons: rub the baguette with the garlic clove then cut it into a small dice. Sprinkle it with a little olive oil and spread over a nonstick baking tray. Bake for 5 minutes until golden brown. Set aside to cool.

Finely chop the tongue, mix with the capers, croutons, parsley, salt, and pepper, adding a little olive oil.

Put a spoonful in each pastry case and serve.

Tartlets of chopped beef cheek

Beef cheek is ideal for this recipe as it cooks down beautifully with long, slow cooking, but if you can't find any, use ground beef and assemble like mini shepherd's pies.

Preparation time: 30 minutes
Cooking time: 3 hours

2 tbsp olive oil
3 lb beef cheek (or ground beef)
3 carrots, diced
2 celery sticks, sliced
Thyme, bay leaf
1 bottle wine
1 onion, studded with 2 cloves
7 to 8 large potatoes, peeled
⅔ cup heavy cream
2 tbsp salted butter
Worcestershire sauce or mustard
18 pastry shells
½ cup Gruyère cheese, grated
Salt and pepper

Heat the oil in a cast iron saucepan and lightly brown the beef all over. Add the vegetables and herbs, and cook a few minutes longer. Add the wine, onion, and a little salt and pepper (not too much, as the liquid will reduce a lot). Cover and cook over a low heat for at least 3 hours. Add water if necessary to prevent drying. Boil the potatoes until well-cooked then mash or purée them with the cream, butter, and seasoning.

Dice the meat, season with salt, pepper, and Worcestershire sauce or mustard. Place a little meat in each pastry shell, cover with potato purée, and sprinkle with Gruyère cheese.

Reheat in the oven at 350°F for 4 to 5 minutes before serving.

Mini bouchées à la reine…almost

This is a little twist to the traditional filling for vol-au-vents, light puff pastry shells that resemble small pots with lids. Bouchées are little "mouthfuls" with savory fillings.

Makes 18 mini vol-au-vents
Preparation time: 20 minutes

3½ tbsp unsalted butter
2 tbsp all-purpose flour
4 cups chicken stock
5 boneless, skinless chicken breasts, lightly poached and diced
⅔ cup small white mushrooms, finely sliced
⅓ cup crème fraîche
Sea salt and pepper
18 small flaky pastry vol-au-vent cases (or puff pastry shells about 1½ inches in diameter, 1 inch in height)

Melt the butter in a saucepan, add the flour, and cook gently for several minutes, stirring constantly. Pour in the chicken stock and bring to the boil. Add the chicken and mushrooms, and cook for another 10 minutes. Add the crème fraîche, season to taste, and fill the pastry cases (preheated for 5 minutes).

You can prepare the sauce in advance, filling the pastry cases just before serving, in which case, they should be reheated gently for 5 minutes.

Navy beans with garlic and Parmesan rind

Serves 6 to 8
Preparation time: 10 minutes
Cooking time: 25 minutes

4¼ tsp butter
1 tbsp olive oil
2 garlic cloves, finely chopped
2 shallots, finely chopped
1 can (15 oz) navy beans, drained and rinsed, or 7 oz dried navy beans soaked overnight then rinsed and boiled for 30 minutes or until just soft, not mushy
4 cups chicken or vegetable stock
3½ tbsp Parmesan rind

Melt the butter in the oil then add the garlic and shallots, and let sweat for a few minutes. Add the other ingredients, bring to the boil, and cook for 20 to 25 minutes.

Remove the Parmesan rind, blend the soup in a food processor, and season. Serve or set aside, and reheat gently when ready to serve.

Spinach and potato

Serves 8
Preparation time: 10 minutes
Cooking time: 30 minutes

2 tbsp olive oil
1 onion, finely chopped
Handful of Italian parsley, chopped
3½ cups hot vegetable stock
2 waxy potatoes, sliced
1 lb fresh spinach
2 Granny Smith apples

Sweat the onion in a pan without browning, add the parsley, and cook for 1 minute. Add the hot stock and the potatoes, and cook for 10 minutes.

Add the spinach and cook for another 15 minutes. Blend in a food processor. Reheat the soup and pour into bowls. Top with the grated apples before serving.

Leek and orange

Serves 8
Preparation time: 10 minutes
Cooking time: 30 minutes

2 tbsp olive oil
2 onions, finely chopped
2 celery sticks, chopped
3⅓ cups leeks, white part, chopped
3½ cups vegetable or chicken stock
See Creamed petit pois (see p. 38) for a quick stock recipe
Heavy cream
Juice and grated rind of 1 orange

In a saucepan, let the vegetables color in the oil without browning. Add the stock and cook for around 20 minutes, until the vegetables are soft. Blend with a mixer or food processor then stir in the cream followed by the orange juice and grated rind. This will make the soup deliciously creamy.

Garlic and almond cream

Serves 8
Preparation time: 10 minutes
Cooking time: 30 minutes

10 garlic cloves
6 slices French bread, crusts removed
1¼ cups milk
1⅓ cups almonds, blanched and ground
2 cups water (approximately)
Salt and pepper

Preheat the oven to 375°F and roast the unpeeled garlic for 25 minutes. When cool, squeeze out the pulp.

Soak the bread in the milk for a few minutes. Add the garlic pulp and the almonds and enough water to obtain a creamy consistency. Season to taste.

Serve chilled or reheat gently before serving with a few drops of olive oil and croutons made with buttered bread.

Roast vegetables with basil and olive oil

Pecorino, lemon, and crème fraîche

Roast vegetables with basil and olive oil

Serves 6
Preparation time: 10 minutes
Cooking time: 35 minutes

1 eggplant
1 zucchini
2 tomatoes
1 onion
1 red bell pepper
4 tbsp olive oil
2 to 3 tbsp fresh basil
Salt and pepper

Preheat the oven to 350°F.

Cut the vegetables into chunks. Pour the olive oil over and roast for about 35 minutes.

Season and stir into the pasta. Sprinkle with basil.

Pecorino, lemon, and crème fraîche

Serves 6
Preparation time: 10 minutes

¾ cup pecorino cheese, grated
Grated rind of 2 lemons
1½ cups heavy cream
Salt and pepper

Mix the cheese with the grated lemon rind and cream. Heat gently, season to taste, and pour over pasta.

Broccoli, pine nuts, and mascarpone

Serves 6
Preparation time: 5 minutes
Cooking time: 15 minutes

1 cup pine nuts
2 heads fresh broccoli
1¼ cups mascarpone cheese
Salt and pepper

Broil or lightly brown the pine nuts in a pan and set aside.

Steam or boil the broccoli then break into florets. Stir into pasta with half the pine nuts and the mascarpone. Garnish with the remaining pine nuts and serve immediately.

A good tomato sauce

Serves 6
Preparation time: 15 minutes
Cooking time: 25 minutes

1 tbsp olive oil
1 garlic clove, crushed
1 lb well-ripened tomatoes or 24 to 25 oz canned tomatoes, seeded, and roughly chopped
1 tbsp parsley, chopped
1 tbsp basil, chopped
1 tsp sugar
1 tsp concentrated tomato paste
2 tbsp red wine
Parmesan or pecorino cheese
Salt and black pepper

Heat the oil in a pan and cook the garlic briefly, add the tomatoes, herbs, and sugar.

Simmer for 10 minutes then add the tomato concentrate and the wine. Cook for another 15 minutes. Season to taste, and serve with pasta or a roast. Serve dish with a bowl of freshly grated Parmesan or pecorino for diners to help themselves.

Tip • Make 'homemade' tomato concentrate by mixing sun-dried tomatoes into pasta.

Broccoli, pine nuts, and mascarpone

Baked apples with cinnamon butter and brown sugar

Serves 6
Preparation time: 10 minutes
Cooking time: 30 minutes

6 cooking apples
¾ cup butter, softened
1 tbsp cinnamon
3 tbsp brown sugar

To serve:
Mascarpone cheese
Seeds from 1 vanilla bean

Preheat the oven to 350°.

Mix the butter with the cinnamon and sugar. Core the apples, but not quite through or the filling will leak out. Run the point of a sharp knife round each apple to prevent it from bursting while cooking. Fill the apples with the spicy, butter mixture and bake for about 30 minutes. Serve hot with vanilla mascarpone (mix the seeds from a vanilla bean into 4 to 5 tablespoons mascarpone).

Ice cream with bread crumbs and caramel sauce

Serves 10
Preparation time: 15 minutes

1 quart good vanilla ice cream
4 slices white sandwich bread, crusts removed

Remove the ice cream from the freezer to soften.

Toast the bread lightly and leave to cool. Using a food processor or your fingers, crumble the bread finely and mix into the ice cream. Return to the freezer until firm.

Serve with caramel or fudge sauce.

French bread pudding

Serves 6
Preparation time: 10 minutes
Resting time: 20 minutes
Cooking time: 40 minutes

6 or 7 slices of day-old white sandwich bread, crusts removed
2 cups milk
2 cups heavy cream
¼ cup sugar
2 whole eggs, plus 3 yolks
1 vanilla bean, split in two
½ cup raisins

Preheat the oven to 325°F.

Cut the bread in pieces and put in an ovenproof dish.

Whisk the eggs and sugar until the mixture turns pale and foamy. Meanwhile, put the milk and cream into a saucepan, add the vanilla bean, and bring to a boil.

Remove the vanilla bean and pour the hot milk over the eggs, stirring well.

Scrape out the vanilla bean and add the seeds to the milk-egg mixture. Add the raisins and pour over the bread, leave to swell for 20 minutes.

Cook for about 40 minutes. Serve warm or cold.

Pear and cranberry crumble

Serves 6
Preparation time: 15 minutes
Cooking time: 45 minutes

6 to 7 tbsp granulated sugar
1 cup all-purpose flour
¾ cup butter
5 ripe pears, peeled and diced
⅔ cup cranberries
2 to 3 tbsp dark brown sugar

Preheat the oven to 375°F.

In a large bowl, rub the sugar, flour, and butter through your fingers until the mixture resembles bread crumbs.

Put the pears and the cranberries in an ovenproof dish, sprinkle with the crumble mixture, and the sugar.

Bake in the oven for about 45 minutes.

Best of British

Host a party with a different flavor and get away from all those fusion, Asian, or Italian menus.

Guests will love this version of British cooking, sweeping away long-held prejudices formed during their first trips abroad.

There's great scope for dressing-up, too: any style, from the old-but-good-kilt-I-couldn't-bear-to-throw-out to the 'we will always love you Lady Diana' T-shirt, not to mention the latest creations of Burberry, Paul Smith, or Galliano.

Have some fun with it and create your own favorite British look!

Royal Pimms

Summer fruits (e.g., strawberries, raspberries, cherries)
Sprigs of mint
1/3 Pimms (aromatics-infused,
gin-based liquor)
2/3 champagne
Ice cubes

Put the fruit in a tumbler. Pour the Pimms
over the fruit then add the champagne,
ice cubes, and mint. Serve immediately.

Beef and horseradish

Makes 12 small sandwiches
Preparation time: 5 minutes

3 to 4 tsp of horseradish sauce or 3 tsp of crème fraîche or mascar-pone cheese mixed with 1 tsp of puréed horseradish
3½ oz cooked roast beef, sliced very thinly
6 slices of bread (e.g., white, brown, whole wheat)

Spread the horseradish sauce on 3 slices of bread. Put a slice of beef on each, and top with the remaining 3 slices of bread. Cut off the crusts and cut the sandwiches into 4 triangles or fingers.

Double salmon

Makes 12 small sandwiches
Cooking time: 2 minutes
Preparation time: 5 minutes

5 oz salmon fillet, steamed or microwaved
2 oz smoked salmon
1 tbsp crème fraîche or mascarpone cheese
2 tbsp lemon juice
1 tsp dill, chopped
1 tsp chives, chopped
6 slices bread (e.g., white, brown, whole wheat)

Chop all the salmon and mix with the crème fraîche, lemon juice, and herbs.

Spread on 3 slices of bread, top with the other slices, remove crusts, and cut into 4 triangles or fingers.

Ham and cheddar

Makes 12 small sandwiches
Preparation time: 5 minutes

3½ tbsp unsalted butter, softened
6 slices bread (e.g., white, brown, whole wheat)
3 slices ham
⅔ cup cheddar cheese, finely sliced

Butter 3 slices of bread. Lay a slice of ham on each then a slice of cheese. Top with the remaining 3 slices of bread. Remove the crusts and cut into 4 triangles or fingers.

Corned beef with two tomatoes

Makes 12 small sandwiches
Preparation time: 10 minutes

1 tomato
1 sun-dried tomato in oil
1 small can corned beef, finely chopped
2 tbsp Worcestershire sauce
6 slices of white bread
Sea salt and pepper

Plunge the fresh tomato into boiling water for 30 seconds, then into cold, and peel. Chop finely with the semi-dried tomato and mix with the corned beef. The juice and oil of the tomatoes will give the mixture a smooth texture. Season with salt, pepper, and Worcestershire sauce.

Spread on 3 slices of bread and cover with the remaining 3 slices. Remove the crusts and cut into 4 triangles or fingers.

Dressed crab

Dressed crab with yogurt, cilantro, and lime on arugula and baby spinach salad with Melba toast

Ah, Melba toast, that inspired creation by famous French chef Auguste Escoffier for Australian opera singer, Dame Nellie Melba. So hip in the 1970s, it looked tasty, but was impossible to butter. Nowadays it's retro enough to make a comeback.

Not so long ago, my Northern Irish compatriots disliked cooking or preparing fish and seafood. They always bought it filleted and pan-fried or 'dressed' it – hence the name of this dish. For this recipe, if you are cooking for many, it will save time if you buy crabmeat already taken off the shell.

Serves 6 as a small starter
Preparation time: 25 minutes
Resting time: 30 minutes

⅔ cup (about 5 oz) crabmeat
2 tbsp natural Greek yogurt
2 tbsp fresh cilantro, finely chopped
1 tbsp fresh basil, finely chopped
Juice of ½ lime
1½ tbsp shredded coconut
3 slices of day-old white bread
A few handfuls of arugula and baby spinach
Sea salt and pepper

Preheat the broiler.

Mix together the crabmeat, yogurt, herbs, lime juice, and coconut, and season.

Set aside for 30 minutes to let the herbs diffuse their aromas.

Remove the crusts from the bread and toast both sides lightly under the broiler. Using a sharp knife, cut through each slice horizontally. This is a rather delicate operation, but don't panic if they don't come out as 6 perfect thin slices. You will be breaking them up afterwards. Just make sure that they're big enough to retrieve if they get stuck on the broiler rack.

Put the untoasted sides under the broiler and toast lightly. Set aside to cool.

Put a few salad leaves in glasses or bowls, add ½ tablespoon of the crabmeat mixture to each, top with a piece of Melba toast, and serve.

Ploughman's lunch

How rare it is to find this great pub specialty served up as it should be: a big plate of carrot and celery sticks, decent cheese, homemade chutney, pickled onions, and good bread. It's a very practical starter, just provide the complete spread so that everyone can make their own sandwiches or simply munch a few crudités.

Serves 10
Preparation time: 20 minutes

4 carrots, cut into sticks
4 celery stalks, sliced into sticks
10 small hearts of lettuce
20 radishes
20 small pickled onions
1⅓ cup (10½ oz) Stilton cheese
1⅓ cups (10½ oz) cheddar cheese
Butter
5 tbsp chutney
Good bread hand-pulled apart or cut into rustic chunks

Arrange all the ingredients on a board or a pretty platter.

Remember to provide knives and small plates so that all can help themselves.

Cheesy potato with cheddar and sweet corn

Makes 20 portions
Cooking time: 25 minutes
Preparation time: 20 minutes

10 small firm-fleshed potatoes
1 medium can whole kernel sweet corn
7 oz grated cheddar cheese
3½ tbsp butter, melted
Salt and pepper

Boil the potatoes unpeeled.

When cooked, slice in half and take out a little of the potato to make a small well in the center. Cut a sliver from the uncut side of each potato so that they will stand firm. Mix the potato with the corn, cheese, and butter. Season, and top each half-potato with a spoonful of the mixture, then brown for 3 minutes under the broiler.

Cheesy potato with cheddar and sweet corn

Bloody Mary soup

Serves 8
Cooking time: 50 minutes
Preparation time: 10 minutes

2 lb ripe tomatoes, peeled
2 celery sticks, sliced
1 tbsp sugar
Olive oil
2 tsp concentrated tomato paste
Vodka
Tabasco Sauce
Worcestershire sauce
Sea salt and black pepper

Put the tomatoes in a bowl with the celery and sugar, and season lightly. Cover and leave to marinate for about 40 minutes then add the tomato paste and olive oil. Blend with a mixer or food processor, adding a little water if the soup is too thick.

Chill well before adding vodka to taste.

Serve chilled with celery sticks. Your guests may season to taste with Tabasco, Worcestershire, salt, and pepper.

Partan bree

This is a traditional Scottish soup that requires some work in removing the crabmeat from its shell. It's not too difficult, however.

Serves 8
Cooking time: 30 minutes
Preparation time: 25 minutes

1 cooked crab, weighing about 3 to 4 lb
1 celery stick, diced
1 carrot, cut into rounds
1 turnip, halved
2 shallots, finely chopped
3½ tbsp long-grain rice
2 cups milk
2 cups heavy cream
1 tbsp Worcestershire sauce
2 or 3 tsp Scotch whisky (optional)

Extract the crabmeat from the shell and set aside. Put the carcass in a saucepan with the vegetables, cover with water, and simmer for about 25 minutes.

Pass the crab stock through a fine sieve then reduce by boiling if necessary to obtain 2 to 3¼ cups (17–25 oz) of stock. Reserve several pieces of the claws for decoration.

Simmer the rice and milk in another saucepan for about 20 minutes, until all the milk is absorbed. Put in a food processor along with the crabmeat and stock, and process well.

Before serving, add the cream and season to taste. Add the Worcestershire and whisky, and reheat gently. Decorate with meat from the crab claws and serve with Scottish oatcakes or toasted oat crackers.

Cream of petits pois with almonds, buttered toast, and preserved lemon

Serves 6
Preparation time: 30 minutes
Cooking time: 10 minutes

For the soup:
4½ lb fresh unshelled petits pois (small, young green peas) or
1 lb frozen petits pois
4 cups chicken or vegetable stock
3½ tbsp whole almonds, blanched, and peeled
⅔ cup heavy cream

For the toast:
⅔ cup unsalted butter, softened
3½ tbsp preserved lemon, finely chopped
15 small slices crusty French bread
1 or 2 sprigs of chervil, to decorate

Shell the peas and cook in the stock for 10 minutes; if frozen, cook as indicated on the package.

Add the almonds and blend the soup well in a food processor. Stir in the cream, adding water if necessary to adjust the consistency.

Mix the butter with the lemon. Serve it in a pretty butter dish with the toast and let everyone help themselves.

This soup can be made ahead of time and reheated before serving. Decorate with several sprigs of chervil.

Tip • Chicken stock gives the best flavor. But if you have neither a chicken carcass nor time in hand, you can make an 'express' stock with 8 cups of water, 1 carrot, 1 stick celery, 1 onion, and a bay leaf. Peel and dice the vegetables then boil over a high heat for at least 30 minutes. Press through a fine sieve before using. This better suits the delicate petits pois and almonds than a stock cube or powder.

Parsnip and apple soup with saffron and cumin

Parsnip's sweetish taste, halfway between carrot and celeriac, goes well with spices.

Serves 6
Preparation time: 15 minutes
Cooking time: 50 minutes

1 pinch saffron
3½ oz onions, diced
2 tbsp olive oil
3½ cups (1¾ lb) parsnip, peeled and diced
4 cups water
1 cup apples, peeled and diced
2 tsp cumin
Salt and pepper

Soak the saffron in 2 tablespoons of hot water.

Heat the olive oil in a saucepan and sweat the onions. Add the parsnip and cook a few minutes longer, then add the water. Cook for 30 minutes more, add the apples, and cook for another 10 minutes. Take off the heat, blend in a food processor, add the saffron water, and cumin. Add more water if the mixture is too thick. Season to taste and serve.

Coronation chicken

Beef and beer ragout with cheddar croutons

Breakfast omelet

Coronation chicken

This is my version of a dish created to mark the Coronation of Queen Elizabeth II. It's delicious and very practical.

Serves 6
Preparation time: 10 minutes
Cooking time: 20 minutes
Chilling time: 30 minutes

2 bay leaves
1 stick celery
1 carrot, diced
1 small onion
2 cups white wine
2 cups water
6 boneless, skinless chicken breasts
Salt and pepper

For the sauce:
2 tbsp mayonnaise
1 cup heavy cream
1 tbsp sun-dried tomato paste
1 to 2 tbsp curry sauce (preferably korma or tikka)

Bring to boil the water, wine, and all other ingredients, except the chicken. Reduce the heat, add the chicken breasts, and poach for about 20 minutes. Remove from the bouillon and leave to cool, and cut into bite-sized pieces.

Mix the sauce ingredients together thoroughly and add the chicken, stirring to coat each piece. Serve chilled, accompanied with basmati rice, flavored with cardamom seeds, and the grated rind of 1 lemon, if desired.

Tip • For the photograph (see p. 40), I decorated the dish with Pan Masala, available from Asian grocery stores.

Beef and beer ragout with cheddar croutons

Serves 6
Preparation time: 20 minutes
Cooking time: 2Ω hours

4 onions, finely chopped
2 lb lean stewing beef, cubed
1 tbsp all-purpose flour
3 tbsp olive oil
2 cups (1½ cans) beer
2 cups water
3 celery sticks, sliced
2 carrots, sliced into rounds
2 tbsp tomato paste
2 bay leaves
1 baguette
⅔ cup (5 oz) cheddar or Stilton cheese, grated
Pinch of salt

To season:
Sea salt and freshly milled black pepper
Worcestershire sauce

Preheat the oven to 300°F.

In a flameproof casserole that you can bring to the table, gently soften and color the onions in the oil then add the meat. When it is browned all over, add the flour and cook gently for another 1 to 2 minutes. Add more oil if necessary.

Add all the other ingredients and mix well, scraping up any sticking to the bottom. Bring to a boil then transfer to the oven and cook for around 2½ hours. Adjust the seasoning with Worcestershire, salt, and pepper.

To make the croutons: 20 minutes before serving, slice the baguette into rounds, sprinkle with cheese, and put the croutons on top of the ragout. Turn up the temperature to 350° and place in the oven for 20 minutes, and serve.

Tip • The ragout can be prepared the night before or served cold. It will only improve. Reheat it before adding the croutons, if you don't want to serve it cold.

Breakfast omelet

Serves 6
Preparation time: 5 minutes
Cooking time: 15 minutes

2 pork sausages, cut into rounds
⅓ lb bacon, diced
4 to 5 small white mushrooms, sliced
2 tomatoes, seeded
8 eggs, lightly whisked
Salt and pepper

Heat a nonstick frying pan and fry the sausages, then the bacon, mushrooms, and finally the tomatoes, cooking each for a few minutes in turn. Then add the eggs, a little salt and pepper, and cook gently for 5 to 7 minutes. Slide the omelet onto a plate and serve hot, warm, or cold.

Stilton terrine with two pears

Serves 6 to 8
Preparation time: 20 minutes
Chilling time: 3 to 4 hours

⅔ cup dried pears, sliced
1¼ to 1½ cups Stilton cheese, crust removed and crumbled
4 to 5 slices whole wheat bread, crust removed
3 ripe pears (e.g., Comice), peeled and diced

Line a small terrine with plastic wrap and place the slices of dried pears neatly along the base, as this will be on top when presented for serving. (Do not use a flexible mold as you want the mixture to be shaped by the sides.)

Divide the Stilton into 2 equal portions and place 1 portion of the cheese in a layer over the dried pears.

Cut the bread to fit, divide into 3 equal portions, and press 1 portion of the bread down firmly over the cheese.

Put the fresh pears on top of this layer of bread, cover with a second layer of bread, and add the second layer of cheese. Finish with a layer of the remaining bread.

Cover with a piece of foil or wax paper, then a piece of stiff card cut to fit. Place a heavy weight (full jars or cans, if you don't have a weight) onto the card.

Refrigerate for at least 3 or 4 hours, overnight if you can.

Turn out carefully from the terrine onto a pretty plate and serve with a crisp green salad, and walnuts or hazelnuts.

Upside-down summer pudding

Real sherry trifle

Christmas pudding ice cream

Upside-down summer pudding

This is a great British classic, not at all like those stodgy boiled pud-dings that have such a bad reputation in France. Here, I've suggested making it in individual portions to save turning out.

Serves 6 to 8
Preparation time: 25 minutes
Cooking time: 15 minutes
Chilling time: overnight

3 to 3½ cups (1½ to 1¾ lb) summer fruits (e.g., strawberries, rasp-berries, blackberries, blackcurrants, cherries, gooseberries); reserve some of the best for decoration
⅓ to ¼ cup sugar, depending on the ripeness of the fruit
8 to 10 slices day-old white sandwich bread, crusts removed
Heavy cream
Mascarpone cheese (optional)

For serving: small individual ramekins or tumblers

Put the sugar and all the fruit, except the strawberries and raspberries, in a saucepan with ½ cup water. Cook gently, stirring until the sugar dissolves. Add the remaining fruits, halving the strawberries if large, and cook for another 5 minutes. The fruit should be poached without losing its shape. Set aside to cool for about 15 minutes.

Cut the bread slices into triangles, and line the bottom and sides of each ramekin. Carefully spoon in the poached fruit.

Chill overnight in the refrigerator.

Decorate with the reserved fruit and serve with cream into, if you wish, 1 tablespoon of mascarpone and a little sugar stirred together.

Real sherry trifle

Serves 8 to 10
Preparation time: 15 minutes
Cooking time: 30 minutes
Chilling time: 3 hours

20 sponge cake ladyfingers
4 tbsp cherry jam
5 tbsp sherry
2 bananas, peeled and sliced into rounds
Grated rind of ½ lemon and 2 tbsp of juice
1 cup pitted black preserved cherries
5 egg yolks
3½ tbsp sugar
2 cups milk
3 tbsp mascarpone cheese
1 cup heavy cream
3 tbsp flaked almonds, toasted

Spread cherry jam on the sponge fingers and arrange them in a pretty dish. Pour the sherry over. Soak the sliced bananas in the lemon juice to keep them from turning brown and layer them on top of the ladyfingers. Arrange the cherries on top.

Beat the egg yolks and sugar together until the mixture turns pale. Bring the milk to a boil, take off the heat, and pour over the egg yolks, stirring constantly. Return the custard to the pan and cook gently WITHOUT boiling, until it thickens. Set aside until completely cold and pour over the fruit.

Whip the cream lightly, stir in the mascarpone, and pour over the custard. Decorate with the almonds.

Christmas pudding ice cream

The pudding flavor mingles with the ice cream for a party dessert that is much easier to make than a real pudding.

Serves 8 to 10
Preparation time: 15 minutes
Steeping time: overnight
Chilling time: 1 hour

2 tbsp candied mixed fruits, diced
2 tbsp candied orange peel, diced
2 tbsp currants
2 tbsp raisins
1 tbsp walnuts, finely chopped
5 tbsp rum
3 tbsp port
Grated rind of 1 orange
Grated rind of ½ lemon and 2 tbsp juice
1 tsp allspice
1 quart good-quality vanilla ice cream

Mix together all the ingredients, except the ice cream, in a large bowl, cover, and leave steeping overnight in the refrigerator.

Take the ice cream from the freezer and let it soften slightly before stirring into the fruit mixture.

Return the bowl to the freezer for 1 hour or so, until the ice cream firms up again.

After Eight mousse...
and matching 'biscuit'

When marketing men, in a frenzy of niche retailing, created After Eight Biscuits, I couldn't resist paying homage to all those restaurant menus with their rather pompous dishes. If you have a hard time finding After Eight Biscuits, substitute with a small-sized wafer or your favorite cookie.

Serves 8 to 10
Preparation time: 10 minutes
Chilling time: 2 hours

1 pint heavy cream
15 After Eight mints, for the mousse
10 After Eight biscuits, to decorate

Bring the cream to boiling point, remove from the heat and beat in the After Eight mints, using a wire whisk, until they are all melted. Chill in the refrigerator for 2 hours.

Whip the mousse with an electric beater until it peaks.

Pour into little cups or ramekins and decorate each with After Eight Biscuits or your favorite cookie.

American favorites

One of my most unforgettable parties is a backyard barbecue thrown in bleak January by Diane, alias Dolly, and Alain, alias Big Al, the celebrated organizers of the first and last genuine Halloween party, three years before the rest of the country sank under a commercial orgy of orange and black plastic.

Sixty-eight people crammed into as many square yards, an enormous margarita was handed to each guest almost before the cars were parked, and a gigantic and efficient barbecue was installed with an outside temperature of 41° Fahrenheit, under a small marquee attached to the French windows of the room set aside for dancing.

Plus, the dressing up involved minimum stress, expense, or feeling foolish. Everyone's got a pair of jeans or a comfortable shirt.

The food is also easy to prepare: good tacos, homemade burgers, and a few ice cream cones. All the same, I have thrown in a few other good ideas.

★

Steak sandwich with BBQ sauce

Serves 8
Preparation time: 20 minutes
Cooking time: 5 minutes

2 (3½ oz) steaks, beaten flat
5 tsp sea salt
2 tsp black pepper
3 tsp ground cumin
1 bottle BBQ sauce
12 thick slices crusty French bread
Olive oil

Coat the steaks with a mixture of the salt, pepper, and cumin, and set aside.

Take half the bread slices and make a hollow in the center of each for the meat. Just before serving, heat the olive oil in a cast iron pan and fry the steaks rapidly, then cut them into bite-sized morsels. Lay them on the bread, anoint liberally with the sauce, and close with another slice of bread.

Cut the sandwiches lengthways into fingers and serve hot.

Nachos

Serves 8
Preparation time: 10 minutes
Cooking time: 10 minutes

2 large ripe avocados, peeled and roughly chopped
1 large tomato, peeled, seeded, and finely diced
4 tbsp lemon juice
1 garlic clove, crushed
1 large bag of tortilla chips
1 large jar salsa, mild or spicy
1 cup cheddar cheese, grated
3 to 4 tbsp crème fraîche or sour cream
Salt and pepper

Prepare the guacamole by mixing the avocado, tomato, lemon juice, and garlic. Blend in a food processor to a smooth purée and season to taste

Preheat the oven to 350°F.

Put the chips in a large ovenproof dish. Pour the salsa over, sprinkle with grated cheddar, and place in the oven, until the cheese melts over the chips. Serve accompanied by the guacamole and crème fraîche.

Lobster roll

On this side of the Atlantic, it may seem rather shocking to use lobster in a hot dog bun with mayonnaise. Never mind, it's delicious.

Serves 4
Preparation time: 25 minutes or however long it takes to extract the lobster meat
Reheating time: 2 minutes for the bread

1 lb lobster meat
1 4-inch celery stick, finely diced
4 tbsp mayonnaise
Grated rind of 1 lemon
4 tbsp lemon juice
4 hot dog buns
Salt and pepper

Mix the lobster meat with all the other ingredients except the buns. The buns should be gently warmed, in the oven or the microwave… whatever's handiest.

Fill the buns and serve.

Peanut butter and jelly sandwich

Some might dismiss this combination as fit only for a child's sack lunch, yet the crunchy, sweet-salty-savory mixture is a classic. Just don't butter the bread before spreading the peanut butter. Enough is enough! While grape jelly is the standard, we liven ours with gooseberry, but any flavor of jam or jelly is fine – it's up to you.

Makes 24 sandwiches
Preparation time: 5 minutes

12 slices of sandwich bread, white or whole wheat
1 jar crunchy peanut butter
1 jar gooseberry jelly or any jelly flavor

Spread the peanut butter on 6 slices of bread and add a layer of jelly. Cover with the remaining 6 slices and cut into four.

Rice salad with black beans and hot salsa

Swordfish ceviche

Prawn, mango, and peanut salad

Rice salad with black beans and hot salsa

Here's a rice salad with a twist…

Serves 10
Cooking time: 10 minutes, for the rice
Preparation time: 20 minutes

2 cans (14 oz each) black beans, or black-eyed peas
1 can (1½ cups) sweet corn
⅔ cup olive oil
1 tbsp ground cumin
5 tomatoes, peeled
2 red bell peppers
5 shallots
2 garlic cloves
2 red chiles
3 tbsp lime juice
2 lb white rice, cooked
1 bunch fresh cilantro, chopped
1 bunch basil, chopped
Salt and pepper

Cook the rice and set aside to cool. Drain and rinse the black beans. Drain the corn. Mix the black beans and corn into the rice, adding 4 tablespoons of the olive oil and cumin. Season to taste and set aside for the flavors to mingle.

Seed the peeled tomatoes and dice the flesh finely. Dice the bell peppers, shallots, garlic, and the chiles.

Mix all the vegetables with the lime juice, the remaining olive oil, and season with salt and pepper to taste.

Arrange on the rice and garnish with cilantro and basil.

Note. If you wish to peel the bell peppers and chiles, roast in a hot oven until the skins blacken and blister. Put in a sealable plastic bag, seal, and leave for about 10 minutes to sweat the skins, which should then peel easily. If you don't want the salsa too hot, seed the chiles.

Swordfish ceviche

Serves 8 (as a starter)
Preparation time: 45 minutes

14 oz swordfish or tuna – tell your seafood market you want to serve it raw, to ensure it's very fresh
Juice of 3 limes
1 cup red onions, sliced into fine strips
2 red bell peppers, roasted, peeled, seeded, and finely diced
2 tbsp Italian parsley, finely chopped
1 tbsp cilantro, finely chopped
2 garlic cloves, very finely diced
½ red chiles, very finely diced (optional)
2 limes, sliced into very thin rounds, to decorate

Slice the raw fish into thin strips and marinate in the lime juice for 30 minutes.

Mix together all the other ingredients then add the marinated fish.

Serve well-chilled and garnished with slices of lime.

Prawn, mango, and peanut salad

Serves 6
Preparation time: 10 minutes

For the sauce:
4 tbsp mayonnaise
2 tbsp mango chutney
1 tsp cumin powder
1 tsp ground ginger
Juice of 1 lime
Sea salt and freshly milled black pepper

2¼ lb cooked, peeled prawns
1 ripe mango, peeled and diced
1 package lettuce hearts, or 2 Little Gem lettuces
3 tbsp dry-roasted peanuts
1 bunch fresh cilantro

Mix together all the sauce ingredients then add the prawns and mango. Line a bowl with the lettuce leaves and add the prawn mixture.

Sprinkle with peanuts and fresh cilantro leaves.

New England chowder

Serves 6
Preparation time: 20 minutes
Cooking time: 15 minutes

3 shallots
3½ tbsp butter
2 tbsp all-purpose flour
2/3 cup white wine
4 cups good fish stock
2 lb mussels, cleaned
1 dozen clams, cleaned and in their shells
½ lb cod or halibut, cut in pieces
5 tbsp crème fraîche
Salt and pepper

Sweat the shallots in the butter, add the flour, and cook for
2 minutes.

Add the wine and fish stock.

Boil for 2 to 3 minutes.

At this point, you can set aside the bouillon and finish cooking
the chowder just before serving.

Add the shellfish and the fish, and cook for another 10 minutes.
Discard any mussels or clams that have not opened.

Just before serving, add the crème fraîche. Serve with little crackers.
To make a more substantial dish, add steamed potatoes cut into
small chunks.

Extra hot chile

Serves 8
Preparation time: 15 minutes
Cooking time: 1½ to 2 hours

2 tbsp olive oil
2 onions, chopped
4 garlic cloves, diced
2 carrots, sliced
1 tbsp ground cumin
1 tbsp dried oregano
3¼ lb minced lean beef
1 can (14 oz) tomatoes, chopped
1 small can concentrated tomato paste
1 tbsp sugar
2 tbsp good chili powder
½ tsp cayenne pepper
4 cups beef bouillon or stock
1 tsp salt
1 large can kidney beans, rinsed and drained
Parsley
Crème fraîche

Heat the oil in a large saucepan. Add the onions, garlic, carrots, cumin, and oregano. Cook over a low heat for 5 minutes.

Turn up the heat, add the meat, and turn it in the oil. It should be sealed and browned all over.

Add canned tomatoes, tomato paste, sugar, chili powder, cayenne, sugar, the bouillon or stock, and salt. Simmer uncovered for about 1 hour.

When the chile has thickened, add the kidney beans and parsley. Cover and cook for another 10 minutes.

Just before serving, add 1 or 2 tablespoons of crème fraîche.

Tip • Try serving with hot tortillas and bowls of crème fraîche, salad, and grated cheddar cheese.

Pecan and maple syrup tart

Serves 8
Preparation time: 10 minutes, pastry; 10 minutes, filling
Chilling time: 2 hours, for the pastry
Cooking time: 35 to 40 minutes

Short crust pastry:
To make a pastry case about 11 inches in diameter

1 cup + 1 tbsp all-purpose flour
½ cup butter, chilled
2 tbsp sugar
3 to 4 tbsp iced water

Put the flour, butter, and sugar in a mixer and process until the mixture resembles bread crumbs. Add the water gradually, as you may not need all of it, and process for a few seconds more. Do not over-process.

Draw the dough into a ball, put in a sealable plastic bag, and leave to rest for 2 hours in the refrigerator.

When ready to cook, take the pastry out of the refrigerator to soften. Preheat the oven to 375 °F. Roll out the dough and line the baking pan. Return the dough to the refrigerator while preparing the filling.

The filling:
¼ cup melted butter
½ cup sugar
¾ cup maple syrup
2 eggs
1 cup pecan pieces

Beat together the butter, sugar, and maple syrup. Add the eggs, beating continually.

Layer pecans in the uncooked pastry case and pour the filling on top. Spread the remaining nuts evenly over the pastry.

Bake for 15 minutes at 375 °F, then lower the temperature to 350°F for 3 to 4 minutes, and bake for another 25 to 30 minutes.

Cool, and serve warm or cold.

Blondies

Makes 30 squares
Preparation time: 15 minutes
Cooking time: 25 minutes

¾ cup butter, softened
1⅓ cups light brown sugar
2/3 cup granulated sugar
3 eggs + 1 yolk
½ cup crunchy peanut butter
1¾ cups all-purpose flour
1 tsp baking powder
1 bag (12 oz) chocolate chips

Preheat the oven to 350°F. Butter a square or rectangular baking pan. Beat together the butter and the two sugars until the mixture turns pale and creamy.

Add the eggs and the single yolk one by one, beating all the time. Blend in the peanut butter, sift in the flour, and baking powder. Add the chocolate chips, mix well, and pour the mixture into the baking pan.

Bake for 20 to 25 minutes. Take care not to overcook; the Blondies should be deliciously sticky.

Maple syrup pancakes

Most supermarkets stock these pancakes nowadays. I know that the ones in the photograph opposite are British-made, but they're very similar to American pancakes. Just reheat them gently in the oven or under the broiler, and serve with maple syrup and a good vanilla ice cream.

Blueberry cobbler with American crumble

Serves 6 to 8
Preparation time: 10 minutes
Cooking time: 20 minutes

2 cups blueberries
3 tbsp sugar

For the cobbler:
3 tbsp sugar
½ cup all-purpose flour
1½ tsp baking powder
1 egg, beaten
⅓ cup milk

Preheat the oven to 375°F.

Put the fruit in an ovenproof dish and sprinkle with sugar.

Mix together the sugar, flour, and baking powder. Add the egg and the milk, and mix well to obtain a smooth texture.

Spoon over the fruit and bake for about 20 minutes.

colors

It's fun to focus on a color when food shopping. A whole meal – starter, main dish, dessert – can be created from all or any of the colors of the rainbow.

A party, however, hinges on variety and dishes that are easy to serve, but the constraints of color can be an inspiration; they can lead the way to trying new things and to ultra-simplicity.

Nature plays its part, too. Every season has its own color. Black and white for the festive season (caviar, truffles, foie gras, oysters), green for springtime (fresh herbs, petits pois, spring vegetables), pink for the beginning of summer (prawns, rhubarb, strawberries, salmon), and orange for autumn (pumpkins, oranges).

Your guests' color coordination can be minimal. Anyone can dig out a scarf, handkerchief, or tie in the featured hue. As for the décor, monochromatic flowers, fruits, and vegetables on a color-coordinated buffet with white or clear glass crockery will harmonize elegantly with your menus.

Black and white

Shots

A small selection of 'shots', powerful mini-cocktails to down in one gulp, as if you were 18 again.

Black dragon
⅓ whiskey
⅓ Kahlúa
⅓ crème de menthe

Black samurai
1 measure sake
1 dash soy sauce

Black tooth
⅔ whiskey
⅓ cup Coca-Cola

Black orchid
⅓ grenadine
⅓ white rum
⅓ curaẏao

Cheeses and dried fruits
Corsican or Basque Tome cheese, black cherry jam
Quail eggs with poppy seeds
Oysters with caviar

Appetizers

Corsican or Basque Tome cheese, black cherry jam

Serve this in 'kit' form. Provide small chunks of bread and serve the jam in a little bowl with a spoon, and the cheese with a knife, so that everyone can dig in as they please. If you can't get Tome, use goat cheese or Lancashire.

Quail eggs with poppy seeds

Quail eggs
Poppy seeds
Sea salt

Hard-boil the eggs.

Peel off the tops. Serve accompanied by a bowl of poppy seeds mixed with sea salt and another small bowl for the eggshells.

Oysters with caviar

For 24 oysters
3½ tbsp (2 oz) caviar – more if your budget permits.

Open the oysters. Arrange them on a bed of black or white pebbles, or even coarse salt.

Top each oyster with a few grains of caviar.

Foie gras morsels

Fill a small spoon with aspic topped with a mouthful of raw or partly cooked foie gras.

Sprinkle with sea salt and pepper.

Salt cod purée (brandade) and pepper sandwiches

1 pot of brandade or smoked mackerel pâté
6 slices white sandwich bread

Spread the brandade on the bread, remove the crusts, and cut into long slices.

Sprinkle with pepper – perhaps a bit less than in the photograph! Brandade is a purée made from salt cod.

Tapenade sandwiches

Makes 20 sandwiches
10 slices white sandwich bread
1 small pot tapenade (black olive purée)

Spread the tapenade in a light layer on half of the bread. Top with the rest of the bread, cut off the crusts, and slice the sandwiches lengthways into fingers.

Rice cakes with black radish

Makes10 cakes
10 rice cakes
1 black radish (more, depending on size)
⅔ cup butter

Slice the radish in very thin rounds. Butter the rice cakes and arrange the radish slices artistically on them.

Roasted, rolled eggplant with tomato and cream cheese

2 to 3 large eggplants
1 jar tomato conserve
1 carton Saint-Moret or Philadelphia cream cheese

Roast the eggplants in a hot oven until cooked through but not mushy. Let cool completely and then cut into slices.

Spread a little tomato conserve over. Not too much, so that the red doesn't show.

Spread with cheese, roll up, and close with a toothpick.

Rollmops

Makes 12 rollmops
1 jar plain rollmops (Bismarck herring fillets wrapped around onion)
12 toothpicks

Cut the fillets into slices then roll them around the little pickled onions that they come with, or buy loose herring fillets from a deli counter and a jar of pickled onions.

Foie gras morsels

Rice cakes with black radish

Salt cod purée (brandade) and pepper
sandwiches + Tapenade sandwiches

Roasted, rolled eggplants with
tomato and cream cheese

Cream of cauliflower with
horn of plenty mushrooms

Potato soup with truffle butter

Cream of cauliflower with horn of plenty mushrooms

Serves 8
Preparation time: 15 minutes
Cooking time: 25 minutes

1 large cauliflower divided into florets or 1 large package frozen cauliflower florets
2/3 cup (5 oz) fresh exotic mushrooms (horn of plenty or chanterelles) or around 3½ tbsp dried, rehydrated
3 shallots, finely chopped
3½ tbsp butter
Milk or water
Heavy cream
Salt and pepper

Boil or steam the cauliflower florets until well done.

Blend the florets, adding enough milk or water to obtain a soupy consistency. Season to taste.

Just before serving, brown the mushrooms and shallots lightly in the butter. Stir a little cream into each bowl of hot soup and top with a spoonful of the mushrooms and shallots.

Cream of asparagus with lemon

Serves 8
Preparation time: 15 minutes
Cooking time: 20 minutes

3 bundles fresh white asparagus or 2 packages frozen white asparagus
4 cups chicken stock
4 cups water
1 cup heavy cream
Grated rind of 2 lemons
Sea salt and pepper

Peel the asparagus, if using fresh.

Cook in the stock and water.

When cooked, blend in batches in a food processor, using sufficient amounts of the cooking liquid to make a soup consistency. Add the cream, stir in the lemon rind, and season to taste.

Potato soup with truffle butter

I detest culinary snobbery, but I strongly advise you to buy only good, fresh truffles.

A perfectly fresh, good quality truffle is more economical as it is extremely powerful. The aroma is so strong that one or two grated slivers will deliver a fabulous taste. To go with it, I prefer simple accompaniments: hard-boiled or scrambled eggs, creamed potatoes or potato soup, raw scallops, or bread, butter, and sea salt.

Beware of the truffles long-frozen and steeped in port that are sold in some delicatessens. Avoid the Christmas period when prices soar. Only truffles gathered less than 10 days earlier and carefully conserved will keep their aroma intact. If you live a long way from a truffle region, ask your gourmet grocer to order or choose a fine one just for you from the shop's supplier.

Makes 12 small bowls
Preparation time: 30 minutes
Cooking time: 30 minutes

2 onions, finely chopped
Nugget of butter
1⅔ lb potatoes
2 cups chicken or vegetable stock
1 pint milk
½ fresh black truffle, weighing 1 to 1½ oz
1 cup good salted butter, softened
½ cup heavy cream
Sea salt

Cook the onions gently in the butter without letting them brown.

Add the potatoes and cook for several minutes, add the stock, and the milk. Cook for another 30 minutes, until the potatoes are well done. Blend the mixture in a food processor, season to taste, and set aside.

Grate the truffle over the softened butter in a small bowl and blend well. Cover with plastic wrap and set aside. Just before serving, gently reheat the soup and add the cream, and then 3½ tablespoons of the truffle butter, blending in well.

Pour the soup into dishes, glasses or bowls, and serve, each garnished with a dollop of truffle butter. Leave diners to add their own salt depending upon how they like to taste their truffle.

Cream of asparagus with lemon

Steamed scallops, mashed potatoes, and black pudding

Steamed scallops, mashed potatoes, and blood sausage

Serves 3 to 6 (depending on how hungry the guests are)
Preparation time: 15 minutes
Cooking time: 30 minutes

6 waxy potatoes
1 small blood sausage
Nugget of butter
½ cup heavy cream
6 scallops

Peel the potatoes and cook in boiling water for 25 minutes or until well done. Mash the potatoes with butter and cream.

Skin the sausage and crumble it over the surface of a heated frying pan.

Cook briskly until it is cooked through and crunchy – but not burnt! Set aside.

Steam the scallops for 3 to 4 minutes. While they are steaming, reheat the mashed potato and spoon into small bowls or plates.

Put the scallops on top of the potatoes, scatter over the black pudding, and serve.

Easy chicken and pasta

This is easier to eat with a fork than those pretty, squid-ink-colored pastas that seem to be everywhere, at least where I shop.

Serves 8
Cooking time: 25 minutes
Preparation time: 20 minutes

1 package wild-mushroom-flavored pasta
4 boneless, skinless chicken breasts
2 shallots, finely diced
1 tbsp olive oil
1¾ cups (13 oz) assorted mushrooms, fresh, frozen, or dried and rehydrated (small white mushrooms, field, chanterelles, oyster, chestnut, trompettes, cèpes…)
1 cup heavy cream
Salt and pepper

Cook the pasta according to instructions on package and set aside.

Poach the chicken breasts for about 5 minutes in lightly salted water, and cut them into bite-sized pieces. Gently cook the shallots in the oil, add the mushrooms, and cook for 10 minutes.

Add the chicken, cream, and warm through if serving immediately. Pour over the pasta and serve.

Everything can be prepared ahead of time and microwaved to reheat just before serving.

Brousse with olive oil

Serves 8
Preparation time: 2 minutes

1 pot of brousse (a Provençal sheep's milk cheese), or ricotta
⅔ cup good olive oil
Sea salt and freshly milled black pepper

Unmold the cheese and serve with the oil, salt, pepper, and a good crusty bread.

Brousse with olive oil

Oreos with coconut ice cream and chocolate sauce

Serves 6
Preparation time: 10 minutes

For the chocolate sauce:
1¼ cups heavy cream
½ cup milk
⅔ cup (5 oz) good plain chocolate (70% chocolate solids)
12 plain Oreo cookies
1 carton good coconut ice cream

Break the chocolate into pieces and put in a heatproof bowl. Bring the cream and milk just to the boil and pour over the chocolate, stirring well. Put aside to chill in the refrigerator.

For the photograph, I split the Oreos and filled them with ice cream, but if you are making large quantities, there's no need to spend ages in the kitchen doing fancy sculptures. Just top an Oreo with a scoop of ice cream, pour the sauce over, and serve.

Meringue with blackberries and blueberries

Makes 10 meringues
Preparation time: 10 minutes

1¼ cups heavy cream
3 tbsp mascarpone cheese
Sugar
Meringues (see p. 112)
1⅓ cups fresh blackberries
1 cup fresh blueberries

Whip the cream with the mascarpone and a little sugar.

Serve the meringues with the cream and fruit on the side, as in an assembly line, and let everyone help themselves.

Meringue with blackberries and blueberries

Floating islands

Lychee and pitaya salad

Floating islands

Serves 6
Preparation time: 20 minutes
Cooking time: 15 minutes

For the custard:
4 cups milk
3½ tbsp sugar
5 egg yolks

For the floating islands:
6 egg whites
3 tbsp sugar

Put the milk in a saucepan and bring it almost to boiling point. Beat the egg yolks and sugar, using an electric beater, until the mixture turns pale and doubles in volume. Pour the almost-boiling milk over, beating constantly. Return the custard to the saucepan over medium heat, stirring constantly with a wooden spoon until it coats the back of the spoon. Leave to cool then refrigerate.

Whisk the egg whites into peaks. Gradually add the sugar, stirring constantly to thicken.

Bring a large saucepan of water to a simmer and poach spoonfuls of whipped egg white by plunging them into the simmering water for around a minute. Drain and set aside to cool.

To serve, pour custard into each bowl and top with an 'island'.

Tip • The egg whites can also be cooked in the microwave. Drop spoonfuls of the mixture directly on the cooking surface one at a time, and cook for 5 seconds at maximum power until the islands puff up a little.

Lychee and pitaya salad

Serves 6 to 8
Preparation time: 5 minutes

1 can lychees
1 pitaya, peeled and cubed (see p. 93 for a photograph of this fruit, found in some Latin markets and specialty markets. If you can't find this fruit, use 6 passion fruits.)

Put some lychees and a little of their juice into each bowl, and add several cubes of pitaya.

Diced pears and a few drops of lychee- or pear-flavored liqueur would go well with this dish.

Poached prunes in Amaretto with ice cream and sweetmeats

Serves 6
Preparation and cooking time: 15 minutes
Chilling time: 30 minutes

20 pitted prunes (preferably pruneaux d'Agen)
⅔ cup Amaretto (almond liqueur)
3 tbsp dark brown sugar
1 carton ice cream, fudge or caramel
A few little marzipan sweetmeats to decorate

Poach the prunes for 7 to 8 minutes in a little water, the liqueur, and sugar, adding more water if they dry out too quickly.

Chill for at least 30 minutes before serving.

Serve a scoop of ice cream with a few prunes and sweetmeats on the side.

Poached prunes in Amaretto
with ice cream and sweetmeats

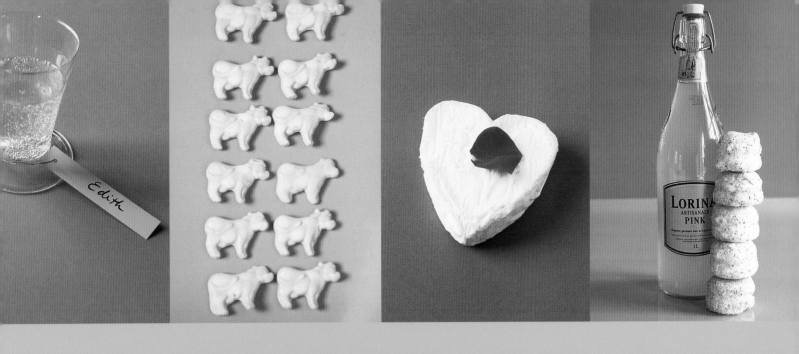

Pink and red

Pink lemonade
with rose water

Add a drop of rose water essence
to lemonade and decorate with rose
petals from your garden (unsprayed
ones, of course!).

Kir royal

Champagne
Raspberry liqueur
Fresh raspberries

Put a raspberry in each glass, add
a drop of raspberry liqueur, and fill
up with well-chilled champagne.

Appetizers

Cracking crisps

Bacon crisps and shrimp crackers have a lovely pink hue. You can't serve enough of them. Intersperse them with homemade creations.

Basket cases

Mix a few shrimp in some mayonnaise with a dollop of ketchup, a splash of lemon juice, and a sprinkle of freshly ground pepper and sea salt. Spoon the mixture into small pastry shells and decorate with a few slices of radish.

Steamy moments

These are delicious and filling, but a bit tricky to cook. You can cook steamed dumplings in a big bamboo steamer (available for next to nothing in Asian markets). They'll look lovely on the table and you can forget about chopsticks.

Fishy tales

Steam red mullet and place slices on rectangles of bread lightly spread with horseradish, brandade, or smoked mackerel paté. Garnish with a twist of lime.

Pink and peppery

Crush pink peppercorns in butter and spread on slices of white sandwich bread. Voilà!

Charcuterie

Choose the prettiest pink cooked meats and salamis from the many varieties available. You can replenish supplies throughout the evening, but do try to present them nicely. Don't make it look too rough and ready, like a picnic.

Tasty taramasalata

Funky, party-pink taramasalata is a perfect canapé food. Don't spend time spreading it on bread or making blinis that end up cold and curling. Just prepare a DIY kit for your guests. Serve it in a bowl, and line up lots of toast and hot blinis. Put them in a cloth napkin to keep them warm.

Scallop and bacon soup

Navy bean and pancetta soup

Scallop and bacon soup

This is a very rich soup; a small bowlful per person is sufficient.

Serves 6
Preparation time: 15 minutes
Cooking time: 15 minutes

2 shallots, finely diced
Nugget of butter
12 to 15 scallops, with or without the stalk
1¾ cups heavy cream
6 slices rindless bacon
Milk
Salt and pepper

Turn the shallots gently in the butter until barely opaque, add the scallops, and fry quickly for a few minutes. Add the cream and heat through blending in the cooking juices. Remove from the heat and set aside.

In another pan, cook the bacon until crisp. Drain on paper towels.

Blend the scallops, shallots, cream, and bacon in a food processor. Add milk or cream until the mixture takes on a creamy consistency.

Reheat very gently before serving.

Navy bean and pancetta soup

Serves 6
Preparation time: 15 minutes
Cooking time: 10 minutes

1 large can navy beans
2 cups vegetable stock
8 thin slices pancetta
1 cup heavy cream
Salt and pepper

Rinse and drain the beans, and put into a large saucepan with the vegetable stock.

Broil the pancetta. Add two slices to the beans and simmer for a few minutes.

Blend in a food processor, add the cream, season, and decorate each portion with a strip of pancetta.

Tartiflette soup

VERY VERY rich. Imagine a rich potato gratin ground and diluted with cream. A little goes a long way. Excellent for a winter party.

Serves 6
Preparation time: 15 minutes
Cooking time: 35 minutes

2 potatoes
1 cup milk
⅔ cup Reblochon cheese
1 cup heavy cream
3½ oz diced bacon

Cook the potatoes in boiling water. When ready, purée the potatoes and add enough milk to give a creamy consistency. Cut the cheese, add, and heat gently until it melts into the liquid. Pour in the cream.

Brown the bacon and add to the soup. Season lightly.

Tartiflette soup

Prawn salad with pink grapefruit and chile mousse

Serves 6
Preparation time: 20 minutes
Cooking time: 5 minutes

20 prawns , uncooked
3 pink grapefruit
1 egg white
3 tbsp mayonnaise
2 tsp dried chiles, finely ground, (preferably the Basque piment d'Espelette, if you can find some)
Sea salt and freshly milled white pepper

Plunge the prawns into a large saucepan of boiling, seasoned water, and cook for 4 to 5 minutes. Cool them by plunging into cold water and peel, leaving the tails intact.

Peel the grapefruit and cut into bite-sized pieces.

Whisk the egg white to a peak, add the mayonnaise blended with the chiles, and season to taste.

Assemble the salad ingredients and pour the sauce mousseline over just before serving.

Chicory and feta salad with pomegranate seeds

Serves 6
Preparation time: 5 minutes

3 heads pink chicory
6 heart of lettuce leaves
8 oz Greek feta cheese
1 pomegranate

Trim the chicory and lettuce, and chop roughly. Dice the feta coarsely, mix into the salad, and sprinkle with pomegranate seeds.

Serve with an olive oil and white wine vinegar vinaigrette.

Crab and pink potato salad with horseradish sauce

Serves 6
Cooking time: 20 minutes
Preparation time: 10 minutes

12 small waxy potatoes
1 tbsp mayonnaise
2 tbsp heavy cream
2 tsp horseradish sauce
1 cup cooked crabmeat, (available vacuum-packed)
Handful of pink peppercorns
Sea salt and freshly milled black pepper

Cook the potatoes, unpeeled, in boiling water. Cool, peel, and slice into rounds.

Prepare the sauce by blending the mayonnaise, cream, and horseradish.

Just before serving, heat up the potatoes in the microwave or by steaming them, then top with the crab, pour over a little horseradish sauce, and sprinkle with pink peppercorns.

Pink coleslaw

Serves 6
Preparation time: 15 minutes

For the salad:
7 oz white cabbage, finely chopped
2/3 cup fennel, finely chopped
15 radishes, cut into rounds

For the vinaigrette:
3 tbsp orange juice
2 tbsp lime juice
2 tbsp soy sauce
1 tbsp sesame oil
2 tbsp rice vinegar

Make the vinaigrette ahead of time.

Assemble the salad just before serving and serve the vinaigrette on the side so that people can help themselves.

Poached salmon in Thai bouillon

Serves 10
Preparation time: 20 minutes
Cooking time: 10 minutes

To make the Thai seasoning:
3½ tbsp fresh ginger, peeled and finely diced
3 garlic cloves, finely chopped
2 lemon grass stalks, finely chopped
2 shallots, finely diced

For the poached salmon:
3 cans coconut milk
4 cups fish stock
Juice of 5 limes
5 to 6 tbsp fish sauce (Nam Pla, Nuoc Mam)
2 tbsp sesame oil
6 to 7 salmon fillets, skinned, and cut into bite-sized pieces
1 lb fragrant Thai rice

Grind the ingredients for the seasoning finely, using a mini-chopper.

Bring to a boil the coconut milk, stock, and the seasoning blend.
Cook for several minutes.

Ten minutes before serving, add the lime juice, fish sauce, and sesame
oil to the stock, and poach the salmon for 5 to 10 minutes. Serve in
bowls with hot rice, cooked according to instructions on the package.

Eton mess (meringue with crushed strawberries)

Pink trifle with rhubarb and white chocolate

Eton mess
(meringue with crushed strawberries)

I'm drawn to dishes with 'mess' in their name. This one is served annually at Eton College.

You could present this dish in 'kit' form, as you would in a 'mess hall'. The pink juice of the strawberries, running into the cream and meringue, has a pretty effect. Gosh, I'm hungry! If using out-of-season strawberries, give them a boost with a little kirsch.

Serves 6
Preparation time: 15 minutes

1 cup heavy cream
2 tbsp mascarpone cheese (not essential,
but it makes the cream particularly creamy)
2 to 3 tbsp sugar
2 cups strawberries
3 to 4 tbsp kirsch if your strawberries are not top-notch
6 meringue shapes (readymade or your own, if you have time.
See recipe below)

Whip the cream until it thickens slightly, adding the mascarpone if desired. Add some sugar. Slice the strawberries, sprinkle with sugar and, if necessary, kirsch. Mix into the cream and, here comes the fun bit, break up the meringues and mix them in, too, to make a lovely, colorful 'mess'.

Meringues

I know that very sophisticated methods exist for making meringues. Some require three hours of cooling in a cold oven or whisking in very precise stages. Here is my recipe for stress-free, perfectly respectable meringues.

Makes about 12 meringues
Preparation time: 10 minutes
Cooking time: 50 minutes

5 eggs
1 cup superfine granulated sugar

Preheat the oven to 250°F.

Separate the eggs. Put the whites in a very clean bowl and whisk with an electric beater. When the whites begin to stiffen, add the sugar, a spoonful at a time, whisking in after every spoonful.

When the meringue is stiff and glossy, drop spoonfuls on waxed paper placed on top of an ovenproof tray.

Cook for about 50 minutes. Remove from the oven and let cool on the tray.

Pink trifle with rhubarb
and white chocolate

Serves 12 to 15
Preparation time: 20 minutes
Cooking time: 15 minutes
Chilling time: 2 hours

2 cups heavy cream
2/3 cup (5 oz) good white chocolate, broken into small pieces
6 to 7 rhubarb sticks, peeled and sliced or 1 cup frozen rhubarb
(less pink, alas)
3 to 4 tbsp sugar
1 package ladyfinger sponge cakes

Bring the cream to boiling point and pour it over the white chocolate. Stir until the chocolate has completely melted into the cream. Chill in the refrigerator for 2 hours.

Poach the rhubarb over a low heat in very little water so that the fruit does not stick to the saucepan. Add sugar, but not too much – the fruit's acidity is necessary to 'cut' the sweet chocolate mousse. The rhubarb should be quite soft.

Whip the cream-chocolate mix until it thickens slightly.

Put a layer of ladyfingers in a serving dish, add the rhubarb, and then add a layer of cream. Repeat once or twice depending on the size of your bowl.

Set aside a couple of sponge cake fingers and crush them to sprinkle on top of the trifle.

Return to the refrigerator for at least 1 hour to let the flavors mingle and the rhubarb juice soak into the ladyfingers.

Lychees and coconut with
pink and white sorbets

This ice cream is irresistible, both for its color and its flavor.

Serves 8
Preparation time: 10 minutes

1 tub each of lemon and raspberry sorbet
20 fresh lychees, peeled or 2 cans, drained
3½ tbsp dried or flaked coconut
Pomegranate seeds (optional)

Put a scoop of sorbet in each bowl, add the lychees, and sprinkle with coconut and pomegranate seeds, if using.

Lychees and coconut with pink and white sorbets

Orange and yellow

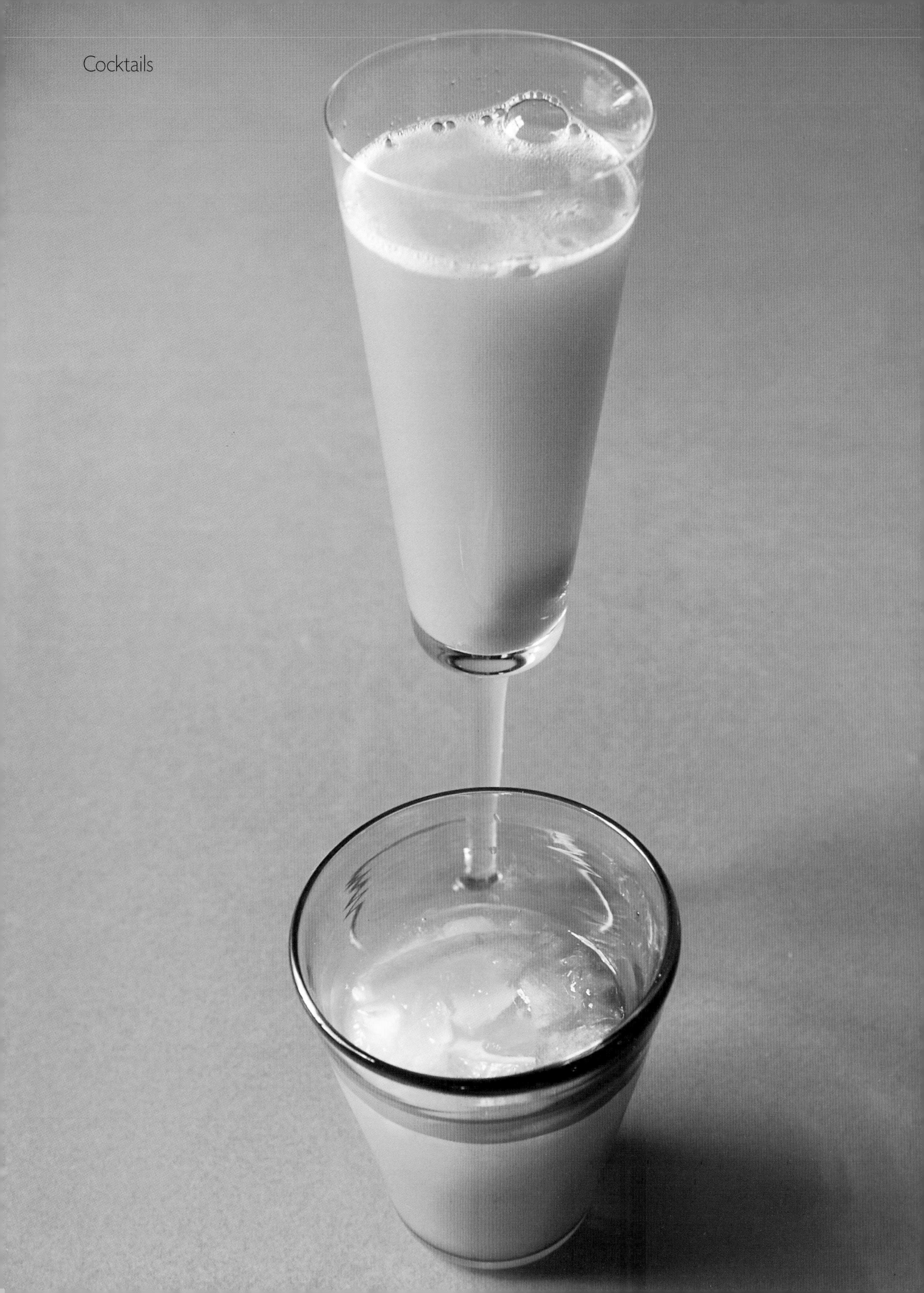

Grand Marnier and orange juice

A great classic: sweet and delicious

²/₃ freshly squeezed orange juice
¹/₃ Grand Marnier
Crushed ice
Orange slices

Apricot cocktail

¹/₃ apricot juice
¹/₃ brandy
¹/₃ champagne
Brown sugar lumps

Mix together the juice and the brandy. Add the champagne and drop a sugar lump in each glass to make the bubbles rise.

Appetizers

Here are a few ideas for the 'I'm-not-cooking-but-I'm-fussy-about-my-orange-presentation' brigade.

Orange and yellow salad
Serves 6
Preparation time: 15 minutes

2 boneless, skinless chicken breasts
2 carrots
1 yellow bell pepper
6 dried apricots
1 preserved lemon

For the vinaigrette:
3 tbsp olive oil
1 tbsp lemon juice
1 tbsp orange juice
Salt and pepper

Cut the chicken breasts into bite-sized pieces.

Shave the carrots into fine strips.

Slice the bell pepper into thin strips. Dice the apricots and preserved lemon finely.

Mix all the ingredients together and hand round the vinaigrette separately.

Hummus with raisins, oranges, and carrots

Preparation time: 15 minutes
Cooking time: 15 minutes

1 can (14 oz) chickpeas
3 tbsp olive oil
Grated rind and juice of 1 orange
2 tbsp tahini
3 carrots, grated
3 tbsp raisins
Salt and pepper

Drain and rinse the chickpeas. Put them in a saucepan, cover with water, and simmer for 15 minutes.

Blend in a food processor, leave to cool then add the oil, orange juice, and rind, tahini, and half the carrots and raisins. Season to taste. Transfer to a serving bowl and garnish with the rest of the carrots and raisins. Ideal for dipping or spreading.

Prawns with cocktail sauce

Serves 6
Preparation time: 5 minutes

1 carrot
18 to 24 cooked, peeled prawns
Small bowl of cocktail sauce (you could make it yourself, but ready-made will go over just as well, so why bother?)

Peel and slice the carrot in half lengthways to use as a stand for the prawns. Arrange the prawns on top.

Serve the sauce on the side and don't forget a little bowl for the tails.

Salmon carpaccio with pink peppercorns

Serves 6
Preparation time: 5 minutes

5 to 7 oz fresh salmon, sliced finely (chill the salmon in the refrigerator or put in the freezer for 30 minutes as this makes the fine slicing easier)
3 lemons, quartered
Sea salt, pink peppercorns, and freshly milled black pepper

Arrange the ingredients prettily and let your guests marinate their own mouthfuls of salmon.

Taramasalata and salmon caviar on black bread

Makes a dozen small slices
Preparation time: 5 minutes

3 to 4 slices black bread
1 pot salmon taramasalata
1 pot salmon roe

Spread the taramasalata on the bread and top with the 'caviar'.

Easy duck with orange

Roast pumpkin with honey, ginger, and cumin

Easy duck with orange

My children prefer my way of preparing this classic dish. It reheats very well, which is useful when you are catering for a crowd.

Serves 8
Cooking time: 2 hours
Preparation time: 10 minutes

2 good-sized ducks
Grated rind and juice of 3 oranges
3 oranges, peeled and segmented, all pith removed
⅓ cup sugar
3½ tbsp butter
⅔ cup chicken stock
Salt and pepper

Rub the duck with the grated rind of 1 orange then tuck it into the cavities. Place them in a large roasting dish and roast at 375°F for 1¼ to 1½ hours.

Remove the ducks from the oven and cut the flesh into bite-sized pieces (not like the photograph!). Set aside. Scrape up the cooking juices and reserve.

Make a caramel by heating the sugar in a heavy-bottomed saucepan. Add the butter, orange juice, and remaining grated rind and the stock. Heat gently until the sugar dissolves anew into the sauce.

Skim off as much fat as possible from the duck's cooking juices. Add the juices to the sauce. Bring to a boil and reduce slightly. Season to taste.

Before serving, add the duck and the orange quarters then reheat the whole dish gently.

Serve with firm-fleshed potatoes.

Tip • If you don't have any good chicken stock handy (99% of the time!) you can get commercial stocks that also thicken the sauce. Unfortunately, they have a very strong and salty taste. The ones I prefer can be bought in liquid form found in small cartons in the supermarket.

Roast pumpkin with honey, ginger, and cumin

Serves 6
Preparation time: 10 minutes
Cooking time: 40 minutes

2 cups peeled pumpkin
4 tbsp olive oil
1 tbsp sugar
1 tbsp ground cumin
1 thumb-sized piece fresh ginger, peeled and finely diced
2 tbsp honey
Salt and pepper

Preheat the oven to 350°F.

Cut the pumpkin into chunks and place in a roasting dish.

In a bowl, mix together the remaining ingredients then pour them over the pumpkin. Turn well to cover the chunks in the oil-spice-salt-sugar mixture then roast for about 40 minutes.

Serve with good crusty, toasted bread and crème fraîche.

Spiced squash soup

Serves 6
Preparation time: 10 minutes
Cooking time: 25 minutes

2¼ lb squash, peeled
2 cups water
1 tbsp ground cinnamon
1 tsp ground cloves
Heavy cream, to decorate
Sea salt and white pepper

Put the squash in a large saucepan with the water. Bring to a boil then simmer gently for about 25 minutes, until quite soft.

Blend in a food processor, adding more water if necessary to improve the consistency. Add the spices and season to taste.

Reheat the soup and decorate with a swirl of cream before serving.

Spiced squash soup

Orange salad with orange-flower syrup

Orange trifle

Orange salad with orange-flower syrup

A classic dish and always delicious. Serve well-chilled.

Serves 6
Preparation time: 20 minutes
Chilling time: 2 hours

6 large juicy oranges with thin skins
1 tbsp orange-flower syrup

Slice 4 unpeeled oranges into thin rounds. Pare the zest from the remaining 2 oranges with a zester, or grate the rind, and squeeze out the juice. Mix zest and juice with the orange-flower syrup

Chill for at least 2 hours.

Orange trifle

Yet another version of trifle, inspired by Boodle's Club in London.

Serves 8 to 10
Preparation time: 15 minutes
Refrigeration time: 6 hours

12 sponge cake ladyfingers (boudoir biscuits)
2 oranges, segmented and cut into pieces
2 tbsp Grand Marnier liqueur, if desired
2 cups heavy cream
Grated rind and juice of 2 oranges
Grated rind of 2 lemons, plus 8 tbsp of juice
1/3 cup sugar

Put the sponge fingers in the bottom of a bowl or glass dish.

Arrange the orange segments over (reserve a few for decoration) and pour in the Grand Marnier, if using.

Whip the cream lightly, add the sugar, grated rinds, orange juice, and as much of the lemon juice as you like. Beat well to incorporate.

Pour over the fruit and leave chilling in the refrigerator for at least 5 hours, to allow the juice to soak into the sponge fingers.

Decorate with orange segments.

Rice with two apricots and vanilla

Serves 8
Preparation time: 10 minutes
Cooking time: 35 minutes

1/2 cup sugar
4 cups milk
3 vanilla beans
1 1/4 cups pudding rice
20 dried apricots, chopped
12 fresh, ripe apricots, pitted and chopped

Pour half the sugar into the milk and bring to the boil. Add 2 vanilla beans split lengthways and the rice, then cook, stirring constantly for about 35 minutes, or until all the milk is absorbed and the rice soft.

Add half the dried and fresh apricots. Press the rice into a ring-mold, cover with plastic wrap, and leave in the refrigerator to chill thoroughly, at least two hours

Put the remaining dried apricots in a saucepan, barely cover with water, and add the rest of the sugar and the third vanilla bean, also split. Simmer to soften the apricots until the water reduces to a syrup. Add the remaining fresh apricots and cook a few minutes longer. The apricots should retain their shape.

Chill and serve with the ring of cold rice.

Rice with two apricots and vanilla

Green

Appetizers

Petits pois and almond hummus

Serves 6
Cooking time: 10 minutes
Preparation time: 5 minutes

1½ cups (12 oz) frozen petits pois (small, young green peas)
1 garlic clove
Juice of 2 lemons or more if necessary
4 to 5 tbsp olive oil
2 to 3 tbsp chopped almonds
2 tbsp almond paste or tahini
Italian parsley, finely chopped
Sea salt and black pepper

Cook the peas in boiling water until soft. Purée the peas in a food processor along with the garlic clove. Add the other ingredients and mix well.

Sprinkle with parsley and serve with flatbread.

Toast with pistachios and almonds

Makes 20 pieces
Preparation time: 5 minutes
Cooking time: 10 minutes

⅔ cup shelled pistachio nuts
⅓ cup almonds, blanched
½ cup Parmesan cheese
2 tbsp fresh basil
3 tbsp olive oil
5 slices white sandwich bread
Salt and pepper

Process all the ingredients, except the bread, in a mini-processor. Spread over the bread and toast under the broiler for a few minutes. Cut the slices into quarters and serve immediately.

Coconut and cucumber rice rolls

Makes 12 rolls
Cooking time: 15 minutes
Preparation time: 15 minutes

3½ tbsp fragrant Thai rice
2 to 3 tbsp coconut milk
1 cucumber
Fresh cilantro
Salt and pepper

Cook the rice in boiling water according to the package instructions. When it is nearly cooked, add the coconut milk, and cook further until it is soft. Season and leave to cool.

Carefully slice the cucumber into long strips, using a vegetable peeler.

Make balls of rice with your fingers and roll the cucumber strips around them.

Secure with a skewer and a cilantro leaf.

Serve with satay sauce (available in supermarkets and Asian markets).

Roast asparagus

When broiled, the little spears of asparagus tips are crunchy and delicious.

Serves 6
Cooking time: 15 minutes
Preparation time: 3 minutes

12 spears green asparagus
2 tbsp olive oil
Sea salt

Preheat the oven to 350°F.

Put the asparagus spears in a roasting dish and drizzle with olive oil. Shake the pan to cover them with oil. Roast for 12 to 15 minutes.

Serve them warm with a light herb mayonnaise or with wasabi, to stick with the green theme. Sprinkle with sea salt.

Mojitos

½ cup white rum
2 tsp sugar
4 to 5 leaves fresh mint
Juice of half a lime
1 slice lime
Ice cubes
Soda water

Put all the ingredients, except the slice of lime and the soda water, in a cocktail shaker.

Mix well, pour into a tumbler, add soda water to taste, and the slice of lime.

Guacamole soup

Serves 6
Preparation time: 15 minutes
Cooking time: 10 minutes

3 garlic cloves, finely chopped
Vegetable oil
2 onions, finely diced
4 cups vegetable stock
Grated rind and juice of 3 limes
5 ripe avocados, peeled, pitted, and cut into pieces
5 tomatoes, blanched, peeled, seeded, and finely diced
1 bunch fresh cilantro, finely chopped
3 corn tortillas
Salt and pepper

Cook the garlic and onion in a pan with a little oil until golden. Add the vegetable stock, lime juice, and the avocados. Bring to a boil then take off the heat and blend in a food processor. Season to taste.

Before serving, reheat gently and add the diced tomatoes, grated lime rind, and the cilantro.

Serve with tortilla slices that have been lightly browned in a little butter.

Chervil and parsley soup

Serves 6 to 8
Preparation time: 10 minutes
Cooking time: 20 minutes

1 bunch Italian parsley
2 bunches chervil
4 shallots, finely chopped
2 tbsp olive oil
Nugget of butter
3 potatoes, peeled and diced
4 cups chicken or vegetable stock
1 cup heavy cream
Sea salt and freshly milled black pepper

Strip off the parsley and chervil leaves, reserving a few chervil leaves for a garnish, and scald briefly, so that they keep their color.

Chop the stalks finely and cook gently in the olive oil and butter, together with the shallots. When they have softened, add the potatoes, and cook for 10 minutes over a gentle heat. Add the stock and cook for another 15 minutes.

Add the parsley and chervil leaves, and cook for another 5 minutes. Serve piping hot garnished with chervil leaves.

If time permits, make little individual salads or present the ingredients separately so that everyone can make their own.

Broiled zucchini with feta and mint

Serves 6
Preparation time: 5 minutes
Cooking time: 10 minutes

3 medium zucchinis or 6 small ones, sliced thinly lengthways
Olive oil
A few sprigs of mint
8 oz Greek feta cheese, crumbled
Salt and pepper

Dry-fry the zucchinis, if possible in a cast iron griddle pan to give pretty stripes. The slices should be thin enough to cook with a quick flash on the broiler, turning once or twice.

Sprinkle with olive oil, salt, and pepper and add the feta and the mint sprigs.

In the photograph, I have used baby zucchinis, found in good supermarkets and vegetable stalls.

Mozzarella, capers, and arugula

Serves 6
Preparation time: 5 minutes

2/3 cup (5 oz) mozzarella di bufala (no excuses, buffalo mozzarella is available everywhere)
2/3 cup (5 oz) arugula
3 tbsp capers
Olive oil
Salt and freshly milled black pepper

Drain the mozzarella and cut into bite-sized pieces, mix with the arugula, sprinkle with capers, olive oil, salt, and pepper.

Fine green beans, steamed mange-tout, and green olives

Serves 6
Preparation time: 5 minutes
Cooking time: 15 minutes

2/3 cup (5 oz) fine green beans
1/2 cup mange-tout (sugar snap peas)
Olive oil
White wine vinegar
Garlic, chopped very finely
3 tbsp green olives
Salt and pepper

Cook the beans and snap peas briefly in rapid boiling water or by steaming. They should remain very crunchy. Make vinaigrette with the oil, vinegar, garlic, salt, and pepper, then stir into the vegetables and add the olives.

Palm hearts, avocado, baby spinach, and lime

Serves 6
Preparation time: 10 minutes

1 can palm hearts
2 ripe avocados
Juice of 2 limes
3 1/2 oz baby spinach
Olive oil
Salt and pepper

Drain the palm hearts and cut into long strips. Peel the avocados, cut into strips, and pour over the juice of 1 lime. Season the spinach shoots with the oil, the remaining lime juice, salt, and pepper. Mix with the avocados and arrange on the palm heart strips.

Fillet of cod, wilted spinach,
mashed potatoes, and chive sauce

Fillet of cod, wilted spinach, mashed potatoes, and chive sauce

This recipe requires two last-minute operations, but they are so simple you can manage easily, even stylishly. For peace of mind, make the mashed potatoes and sauce ahead of time and get the cod fillets ready in the roasting dish.

Serves 8
Cooking time: 30 minutes
Preparation time: 20 minutes

3 lb potatoes, peeled and quartered
2/3 cup heavy cream
1/2 cup butter
8 cod fillets, each weighing about 4 oz
4 tbsp lemon juice
1¾ cups (14 oz) fresh spinach leaves, washed and chopped
1 bunch chives, snipped (reserve 2 tbsp for the sauce)
Sea salt and pepper

For the sauce:
2 shallots, finely diced
3½ tbsp butter
Small glass white wine
2 cups heavy cream
2 tbsp Italian parsley, chopped
Sea salt and pepper

Cook the potatoes in boiling water until they are quite soft. Mash them with the cream, butter, salt, and pepper. Reheat before serving and add the snipped chives.

To make the sauce, cook the shallots gently in a pan with a little butter. When they are soft and transparent, add the wine and simmer gently for around 12 minutes to reduce the liquid. Pour in the cream and stir.

Before serving, reheat and add the remaining butter, stirring lightly to thicken the sauce. Add the parsley and 2 tablespoons of the snipped chives, and season.

Put the cod fillets in a large roasting dish. Pour over the lemon juice and put a small nugget of butter on each fillet. Season lightly. Preheat the oven to 425°F and roast for 5 to 6 minutes. The fish should remain soft and almost transparent.

Meanwhile, heat some olive oil in a pan and rapidly stir-fry the spinach leaves until wilted. Drain well and season to taste. Put a spoonful of spinach on each plate, add a dollop of potatoes, and a cod fillet. Pour the sauce over and serve immediately.

Green chicken curry

If you are short of time, buy a good all-purpose green Thai curry sauce.

Serves 6 to 8
Preparation time: 15 minutes
Cooking time: 25 minutes

To make the green Thai curry paste:
2 lemon grass stalks, chopped
5 green peppers, seeded and finely chopped
2 shallots, chopped
1¾ tbsp fresh ginger, peeled and finely chopped
3 garlic cloves
1 bunch fresh cilantro
2 tsp ground cumin
1 tsp ground coriander
2 tbsp fish sauce (Nam Pla, Nuoc Mam)

2 cups coconut milk
1¼ cups chicken stock
2 tbsp soy sauce
1 tbsp sesame oil
2 tbsp fish sauce
1 lb boneless, skinless chicken breasts, cooked and sliced into fine strips
1 bunch basil, chopped
1 bunch cilantro, chopped

Make the curry paste, by blending all the ingredients in a mini-processor.

Put the paste in a saucepan and cook gently for 3 to 4 minutes, stirring. Add the coconut milk and simmer for 10 minutes then add the stock, soy sauce, oil, fish sauce, and the chicken.

Simmer for 10 minutes longer.

Serve with fragrant Thai rice sprinkled with chopped fresh herbs.

Green chicken curry

Spring vegetable pesto

Serves 6
Cooking time: 15 minutes
Preparation time: 15 minutes

6 good-sized green asparagus spears
3½ oz petits pois (small, young green peas)
3½ oz shelled broad beans
⅔ cup Parmesan cheese, grated
3 to 4 tbsp olive oil
Small bunch of basil
2 tbsp lemon juice
Salt and pepper

Steam or boil the vegetables until they are quite soft.

Cut off the asparagus tips and set aside with a few petits pois and some beans.

Process the remaining vegetables with the cheese, olive oil, salt and pepper, basil, and lemon juice until it forms a thick paste. Add the reserved asparagus tips, petits pois, and beans.

Serve with hot pasta.

Pistachio mousse

Serves 8
Preparation time: 15 minutes

1 cup heavy cream
⅔ cup superfine granulated sugar
⅔ cup pistachio nuts
1 tbsp Amaretto (almond liqueur)
A few drops of natural pistachio or almond essence

Whip the cream lightly with the sugar.

Grind the pistachio nuts into a paste and add the whipped cream, Amaretto, and essence.

Serve in small bowls or glasses with brandy snaps or ginger cookies.

Minty kiwi and cinnamon salad

Serves 6
Preparation time: 15 minutes
Cooking time: 10 minutes

⅔ cup sugar
1¼ cups water
1 stick cinnamon
Few sprigs of fresh mint
12 kiwifruit, peeled and sliced into rounds

Put the sugar, water, and cinnamon stick in a saucepan and simmer gently until the sugar dissolves. Cook for 10 minutes until it turns syrupy. Allow to cool and remove the cinnamon. Pour over the kiwifruit and add a sprig of mint to each glass.

Serve well chilled.

A celebration lunch

Baptisma, communions, weddings…

engagements, Christmas festivities, and Easter lunches. We all need to get together from time to time. When the party is being held at your place, if you are short of experience or inspiration, without access to a caterer, anti-depressants, or your cordon bleu friends, it can sometimes take on dramatic proportions. And even when the members of your family get along as if they were an advertisement for Calvin Klein's 'Eternity', you tend to feel 'on-stage', at the mercy of Great-Aunt Gertrude's inevitable comments. It's difficult to please so many generations and – above all – not to spend five hours at the table on the first fine weekend of the year.

A FEW WORDS OF ADVICE

1 Prepare everything, absolutely everything, in advance. Obviously, this means devoting at least the prior evening to it.

2 Tailor the menu according to whether you will be seated or standing. This makes a difference.

3 Break the ice with your aperitifs, but not your back, or the bank with your dishes.

4 Serve meat or fish as simply as possible, then go to town on the accompaniments. Everyone can dig into what they like and even little Miss Picky (your nephew's vegetarian girlfriend) and James (your brother's 8-month-old son) can feast.

5 A really stylish dessert is indispensable. Nothing marks a traditional celebration better than a superb centerpiece (see p. 7). My advice would be to get a professional caterer, or a pastry shop, to provide a magnificent finale, given that you will have spent less on the other courses. You can simply accompany it with a fresh fruit salad.

Open sandwiches: foie gras and dried apricots; bacon and melon; bacon and oranges; pecorino cheese and chutney

Nectarine and chorizo sausage

Appetizers

Assorted open sandwiches

Let your imagination run riot. Open sandwiches can be varied ad infinitum and feed the hungry without too much work. Here are several sweet – savory combinations.

Foie gras, dried apricots, pepper
Bacon and melon
Pecorino cheese and chutney
Bacon and oranges
Nectarine and chorizo sausage
Cabbage, chestnuts, smoked salmon

Vegetables make great readymade, edible bases. Go for it.

Endives, Camembert, and cranberries

Poach a few cranberries in water. Add a little sugar at the end to reduce their acidity. Fill endive leaves with a bit of Camembert and a few poached cranberries.

Baby bell peppers stuffed with salt cod purée (brandade) or fish pâté

If you can find them, baby bell peppers make delightful multi-colored containers.

Potatoes, horseradish, and smoked eel

Boil or steam the potatoes. Cut in half, spread with horseradish, and top with a strip of smoked eel.

Crackers and oatcakes

Some you can buy, others will be homemade. Don't hesitate to combine readymade products with those you've prepared yourself. You'll be adding a personal touch with your choice of combinations. Here are a few ideas:

Oatcakes or crackers with Parmesan and quince jelly
Bacon and dried pineapple
Mozzarella and balsamic vinegar

Crackers with:
Tomatoes, strawberries, balsamic vinegar
Roast beef, sweet Thai chili sauce

Oatcakes with Parmesan and quince jelly

Endives, Camembert, and cranberries

Open sandwich with cabbage, chestnuts, smoked salmon

Potatoes, horseradish, and smoked eel

Baby bell peppers stuffed with salt cod
purée (brandade) or fish pâté

Crackers and oatcakes

Prune and apple casserole with honey

Roast duck breasts

Roast duck with prune and apple casserole

Serves 12
Preparation time: 15 minutes
Cooking time: 45–50 minutes

6 duck breasts
12 confit of duck thighs (see right-hand column)
6 apples, peeled and quartered (pippin, Braeburn, Granny Smith)
12 prunes, pitted and quartered
4 tbsp fluid honey
Nugget of butter
Salt and pepper

Preheat the oven to 350°F.

Take the duck pieces from the refrigerator 30 minutes before cooking. Put the duck breasts in a roasting dish and cook for 45 to 50 minutes. Test with a sharp skewer.

Put the apples, prunes, honey, and butter in an ovenproof dish. Season, cover, and put in the oven 30 minutes before the duck has finished roasting.

Allow the meat to rest 10 minutes before carving.

Shallot mash

Serves 12

10 floury potatoes
1 cup heavy cream
½ cup butter
6 shallots, finely chopped
Salt and pepper

Put 1¾ tablespoons of the butter in a small saucepan and cook the shallots until golden.

Cook the potatoes in boiling, salted water. Drain and mash well, incorporating the cream and the remaining butter. Adjust the seasoning and add the shallots.

Confit of duck thighs

(Confit of duck thighs is a French specialty. To find it in the U.S., you may have to use a mail order specialty food supplier, unless you have a super gourmet market nearby.)

The objective is to combine the textures of the roast and confit. That way you'll double your chance of pleasing everyone!

I buy my confits! I've made confit of duck once in my life. We had great fun on our little farm but I spent three days at it, until I felt almost preserved myself.

Heat the duck thighs to reduce the fat then reheat again in the oven just before serving, to give a crunchy finish.

Confit of duck thighs

Vegetable gratin + Shallot mash

"Traditional" roast leg of lamb

'Traditional' roast leg of lamb

Serves 8 to 10
Preparation time: 3 minutes
Cooking time: approximately 1½ hours

1 leg of lamb, weighing approximately 4½ lb
5 garlic cloves, peeled and sliced
Large sprig rosemary, leaves stripped and finely chopped
2 to 3 tbsp olive oil

Take the lamb from the refrigerator half an hour before cooking. Preheat the oven to 425°F.

Mix the garlic and rosemary leaves with the olive oil. Score the meat all over and insert the garlic slices. Rub in the olive oil and rosemary. Cook for 30 minutes then lower the temperature to 350°F and cook for 1 hour. The meat can be covered midway through the cooking to ensure that it is cooked through, but some like it quite pink. Check with a sharp skewer.

Slow-cooked leg of lamb

Serves 8 to 10
Preparation time: 3 minutes
Cooking time: 6 hours (at least!)

1 leg of lamb, weighing approximately 4½ lb
5 garlic cloves, peeled and sliced
Large sprig rosemary, leaves stripped and finely chopped
2 to 3 tbsp olive oil

Take the lamb from the refrigerator 30 minutes before cooking time.

Preheat the oven to 225°F.

Prepare the lamb as above and put in the oven. Baste it and cover halfway through cooking time, especially if you are using a fan oven. Don't worry about 'forgetting' it and leaving it to slow-cook. This is a perfect recipe if you have to attend a ceremony before lunch – if you have a cool head, that is. It's what I like to do, although others may prefer to watch over it.

Vegetable gratin

Serves 8 to 10
Preparation time: 15 minutes
Cooking time: 45 minutes for the 'traditional' roast;
2 hours
for the slow-cooked lamb

2 eggplants
4 zucchinis
4 tomatoes
3 onions
Olive oil
4 garlic cloves, crushed
Thyme, finely chopped
Rosemary, finely chopped
Salt and pepper

Slice the vegetables into thin rounds. Layer them in an ovenproof dish, with a little seasoning between each layer, alternating the colors. Drizzle with plenty of olive oil and sprinkle with garlic, thyme, and rosemary. Cook alongside the 'traditional' roast for 45 to 50 minutes. If you are serving with the slow-cooked lamb, it's best to cover the vegetables with cooking foil or to use a covered dish and cook for 2 hours.

Roast poussin and triple-citrus mash

This is a very good way to avoid the problem of ensuring that everyone has a choice of white or dark meat. With a very young, small chicken, everyone gets thighs, breast, or what-they-will. There's no need for anyone to feel put out!

Serves 12
Preparation time: 20 minutes
Cooking time: 1½ hours

6 poussins (small, young chickens)
2 garlic cloves, peeled
Pared rind of 1 lime and 1 lemon (no pith!)
3 tbsp olive oil
15 potatoes, peeled and diced
Grated rind of 3 lemons and 2 limes
1 preserved lemon, finely diced
⅔ cup milk
⅔ cup heavy cream
Sea salt and freshly milled black pepper

Preheat the oven to 375°F.

Rub the poussins with garlic. Tuck the pared rind from 1 lemon and 1 lime inside the 'you-know-where' of each bird (the cavity, if you are still wondering) and season, drizzle with olive oil, and cook for 1 to 1½ hours, depending on your oven's efficiency. Baste from time to time.

Cook the potatoes until soft. Mash with the milk and cream, season with sea salt, and pepper. Add the diced, preserved lemon and the remaining zests, and blend well.

Remove the poussins from the oven and deglaze the roasting dish with a little water, skim off the fat, and reserve the juice.

Serve on a bed of the mashed potatoes and pour over the cooking juices.

Roast poussin and triple-citrus mash

Carrot and parsnip mash

Rolled and tied veal roast

Roast veal with kidneys and carrot and parsnip mash

Serves 8
Cooking time: 3 hours

2 tbsp olive oil
3 lb veal fillet, rolled and tied
1 veal kidney, prepared by your butcher (optional)
Salt and pepper

Preheat the oven to 300°F.

Heat the oil in a roasting pan and brown the veal fillet on all sides. Season lightly and roast for around 2½ hours, basting regularly. If it looks as if it is drying out, cover with cooking foil.

About 35 minutes before serving, turn the oven up to 400°F, sprinkle the kidney with olive oil, and roast whole. (If the veal looks ready during the 35 minutes, take it from the oven, cover with kitchen foil, and keep warm.)

Season and serve with the roast, carrot, and parsnip mash on the side.

Roast veal with kidneys and
carrot and parsnip mash

Everyone loves hash. The following recipes are all precooked (and even minced, which will please those who don't yet have teeth and also those who have dentures). Everything heats up well and can be eaten with a fork.

Preserved duck with chanterelles

Serves 8
Preparation time: 25 minutes
Cooking time: 25 minutes (plus reheating time for the duck thighs and purée)

6 confit of duck thighs (see p. 158)
10 oz chanterelles or other exotic mushrooms
3 shallots, finely chopped

For the purée:
12 potatoes
Butter, milk, cream, salt, and pepper

Heat the duck thighs gently to release their fat.

Remove the flesh and chop into bite-sized pieces.

Make the purée: cook the potatoes and purée with the butter, milk, cream, and seasoning.

Lightly brown the mushrooms and shallots, and set aside.

Make the hash: cover the duck with the potato purée and top with the mushroom–shallot mixture.

If you want to reheat it, the duck and the potatoes can be prepared in advance but the mushrooms should be cooked at the last minute.

Vegetable hash

It's up to you which vegetables to use, depending on the season, the shape and size of your dishes, the number of guests and … anything you like.

Braised veal with orange carrots

Serves 8
Preparation time: 25 minutes
Cooking time: 1½ hours

1 veal fillet
2 carrots, peeled and sliced into rounds
2 onions, finely chopped
2 glasses white wine
Salt and pepper
For the orange carrots:
12 carrots, peeled and cut in chunks
Olive oil
2 oranges, quartered and sliced
Salt
For the purée:
12 potatoes
Milk, butter, cream
Salt and pepper

Preheat the oven to 350°F. Brown the meat in a roasting pan, add the 2 carrots cut in rounds and the chopped onions, then pour over the wine. Season lightly and roast for around 1½ hours.

Put the carrots in an ovenproof dish, sprinkle with olive oil, and a pinch of salt. Roast alongside the meat for the last 40 minutes of cooking time. Remove from the oven and stir in the oranges.

Boil the potatoes and mash to a purée with milk, butter, and cream.

Chop the cooked veal together with the onion and carrots cooked with it, and stir in some of the cooking juices.

Spread a layer of potatoes on top of the hashed meat and top with the carrot–orange mixture.

Shoulder of lamb with chutney

Serves 8
Preparation time: 35 minutes
Cooking time: 2 hours

1 shoulder of lamb
12 floury potatoes, peeled
Butter, whole milk, cream for the purée (optional)
Salt and pepper
For the chutney:
2 handfuls of dried fruits cut in two (prunes, pears, figs)
2 tsp quatre-épices (four-spice blend of white pepper, nutmeg, ginger, cinnamon or cloves)
1 tbsp soft brown sugar
2 apples (preferably pippins or Granny Smith), peeled and chopped
2 pears (Comice), peeled and chopped
2 handfuls of raisins

Roast the lamb, take off all the meat, and chop finely.
Cook the potatoes and mash to a purée with milk, butter, salt, and pepper.

Poach the dried fruits for 5 minutes in a little water with the four-spice mix and sugar. Add the fresh fruit and poach for another 5 minutes or so, until the water evaporates to leave a soft chutney.
Fill a dish or a mold with alternating layers of lamb, puréed potatoes, and chutney.

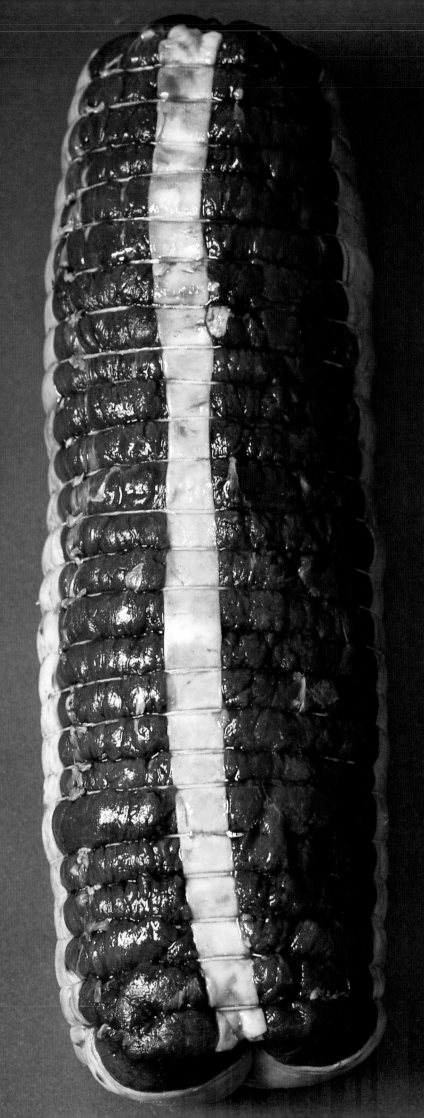

Roast venison

Honey-roast winter vegetables

Roast venison with honey-roast winter vegetables

This makes a great change from the eternal roast: the delicate, unmarinated flavor will please everyone, small and large. Moreover, your butcher does all the work so be sure to give him plenty of notice.

Serves 10
Cooking time: 45 minutes
Preparation time: 15 minutes

3 tbsp olive oil
3 tbsp fluid honey
12 carrots and/or parsnips, peeled and sliced (see photo, p.171)
1 head celeriac, peeled and sliced
Fillet of venison, approximately 4 lb, lovingly prepared by your butcher
Salt and pepper

Preheat the oven to 375°F.

Blend the oil and honey, and toss the vegetables in the mixture. Roast for 40 to 45 minutes.

Take from the oven and set aside.

Forty minutes before serving the meat, preheat the oven to 425 to 450°F. Roast the venison as beef for 30 to 35 minutes until it is well done. Towards the end of the cooking time, reheat the vegetables for a few minutes alongside the meat, then season, and serve together.

Quick-roasted salmon fillets with caper and lemon sauce, and smoked salmon

Serves 12
Preparation time: 10 minutes
Cooking time: 10 minutes

12 salmon fillets, with or without skin
2 cups heavy cream
3 small jars capers, rinsed and drained
3 to 4 tbsp olive oil
2 lemons (to baste the salmon before cooking)
8 oz smoked salmon, diced
24 small potatoes, peeled, steamed, or boiled
3 lemons, quartered (to garnish)
Salt and pepper

Fifteen minutes before cooking, take the salmon fillets from the refrigerator.

Make the sauce by seasoning the cream and heating it with the capers. Take care not to over-season. You will shortly be adding the diced, smoked salmon, which can be salty.

Preheat the oven to 350°F.

Put the salmon fillets in an ovenproof dish. Drizzle with a little olive oil and lemon juice. Season to taste. Cook for barely 5 minutes: the center of the fish should remain moist.

Add the diced smoked salmon to the sauce just before serving, so that it will stay soft.

Serve with the steamed potatoes and garnish with lemon quarters.

There's nothing easier than ordering precooked beef or roasted chicken from your butcher or gourmet market. If you prefer to cook them yourself, here are some recipes to follow.

Roast beef

Serves 8 to 10
Preparation time: 3 minutes
Cooking time: 1½ hours

4 lb beef for roasting
Olive oil
2 onions, quartered
2 garlic cloves, crushed
Salt and finely milled black pepper

Take the roast from the refrigerator 30 minutes before cooking.

Preheat the oven to 425°F.

Heat the olive oil in a roasting pan and quickly seal the meat on all surfaces. Add the onions and garlic, and put in the oven.

Cook for 1 to 1½ hours. In theory, for rare roast beef, allow 25 minutes per 2 lbs meat, plus 15 minutes. In practice, everything depends on your oven. Just keep testing with a sharp skewer, unless you have a meat thermometer.

Set the meat aside to rest and cool completely before carving into thin slices.

Roast chicken

Serves 6 to 8
Preparation time: 3 minutes
Cooking time: 1¼ hours

1 chicken, weighing 3 lb
2 garlic cloves
Olive oil
Salt

Remove the chicken from the refrigerator 30 minutes before cooking time.

Preheat the oven to 425°F.

Rub the skin of the chicken with the garlic, olive oil, and salt. Put a clove of garlic and a little salt inside. Put in the oven and cook for around 1 hour. Baste from time-to-time.

When the chicken has browned nicely, remove from the oven and test by sticking a sharp skewer into the joint between thigh and body. If the juice runs clear, it's done!

Poached salmon

Served 10
Preparation time: 3 minutes
Cooking time: 30 minutes
Chilling time: 2 hours

1 fish kettle
1 salmon, weighing around 4 lb
½ bottle white wine
1 onion
1 to 2 carrots
1 celery stalk
Thyme
Bay leaf
Salt and pepper

Put the salmon in the fish kettle, add the wine, vegetables, herbs, and seasonings. Add sufficient water just to cover the salmon.

Bring gently to a boil. When the water bubbles, turn off the heat and leave the fish to cool until you can test with your fingers.

Remove the salmon, chill it, and carefully remove the skin.

Poached salmon

Caesar salad, French-style

Serves 6 to 8
Preparation time: 15 minutes
Cooking time: 5 minutes

1 baguette
2 garlic cloves, peeled
4 anchovy fillets, finely sliced
4 tbsp lemon juice
4 to 5 tbsp olive oil
4 hearts of romaine lettuce, washed, dried,
and leaves separated
3 hard-boiled eggs, quartered lengthways
1/2 cup Parmesan cheese, grated
Salt and pepper

Preheat the oven to 350°F. Rub the baguette with one garlic clove and cut into crouton cubes. Drizzle a little olive oil over them to coat and bake until golden brown. Set aside.

Crush the remaining garlic and mix with the anchovy strips, lemon juice, and olive oil to make the vinaigrette. Season to taste.

Put the lettuce in a serving bowl and pour the vinaigrette over. Mix well to coat the lettuce leaves. Serve garnished with quartered eggs, Parmesan, and croutons.

TMB

Tomato, mozzarella, and basil: this poor salad has been badly served over the past few years, like tiramisu and carpaccio of beef with pesto. Some restaurants seem unable to do a good job presenting Italian dishes with their delicious combinations of flavors. Nowadays you can buy tomatoes with real taste, mozzarella di bufala, and wonderfully aromatic fresh herbs. Forget rubbery white cheese, frozen basil, and watery tomatoes: this is the real thing, the true taste of Calabria.

Serves 6
Preparation time: 10 minutes

3 balls mozzarella di bufala, roughly chopped
6 ripe tomatoes, sliced
Olive oil
3 to 4 sprigs basil
Sea salt and freshly ground black pepper

Sprinkle the mozzarella over the tomatoes and drizzle the olive oil over. Tear the basil leaves with your hands and scatter over the salad. Season and serve.

Thai cucumber salad

Serves 6
Preparation time: 10 minutes

10 fl oz white vinegar
2/3 cup sugar
2 cucumbers, peeled, seeded, and sliced
2 shallots, finely chopped
2 1/2 tbsp fresh ginger, peeled and finely diced

Mix the vinegar and sugar until the latter has completely dissolved. Add the remaining ingredients. Serve well chilled.

Beets, apples, and celery

When I was a child, we had this salad every Sunday evening. It goes well with cold roast beef.

Serves 6
Preparation time: 10 minutes

2 beets, cooked and diced
2 Granny Smith apples, peeled and diced
2 celery sticks, diced
1 tbsp chopped parsley
Salt and pepper

Mix all the ingredients together and serve well chilled.

Goat cheese with herb 'coulis'

Search out the freshest possible goat cheeses and serve them whole or sliced in rounds, accompanied with cream cheese blended with heavy cream, a little olive oil, and finely chopped fresh herbs (e.g., dill, chives, basil, mint, tarragon).

Roasted goat cheese on a brioche with apple, cranberry, and almond compote

This is a pleasing little variation on the cheese course that saves having to hand around a big platter.

Serves 6
Preparation time: 10 minutes
Cooking time: 10 minutes

½ cup fresh cranberries
2 Granny Smith apples, peeled and diced
1 tbsp sugar
6 slices of brioche
3 crottins de Chavignol or other small rounds of goat's milk cheese
2 tbsp sliced almonds, toasted

Put the cranberries in a pan with a little water and the apples. Poach for 5 to 7 minutes until the apples begin to soften without losing their shape. Leave to cool then add a little sugar – to cut the sharpness of the cranberries and the toasted almonds.

Preheat the oven to 350°F.

Toast the brioche slices and stamp out rounds with a pastry cutter. Cut the cheeses in half and put them in an ovenproof dish. Roast for 2 minutes, remove, place one half on each brioche round, and serve with the compote.

Cheese layer cake

This is a new version of the popular cheese terrine from my previous book *Cooking with Friends* – but with no butter.

Serves 12
Preparation and assembly time: 30 minutes

1 ripe Camembert cheese
1 large tub mascarpone cheese
⅓ cup raisins
½ cup Gorgonzola cheese
2 tbsp poppy seeds
1 small carton Saint-Moret cheese (or fresh, soft goat's milk cheese)
1 white sandwich loaf, thinly sliced and crusts removed
Sea salt and freshly milled black pepper

Mix the Camembert and half the mascarpone with a fork until well blended. Add the raisins and season to taste. Set aside.

Blend the remaining mascarpone with the Gorgonzola and add the poppy seeds.

Work some black pepper into the Saint-Moret or goat cheese. Add salt if desired.

Stack the layer cake, spreading alternating cheeses on the bread, with the goat cheese in the middle and on top.

Neaten the sides. Chill in the refrigerator and serve accompanied by dried fruits and a few sprigs of arugula.

Camembert and caramelized apples

Very, very filling. Eat in moderation.

Serves 6
Preparation time: 10 minutes
Cooking time: 10 minutes

1 ripe Camembert cheese
½ cup sugar
3½ tbsp butter
2 tbsp heavy cream
1 Granny Smith apple, peeled and cut into cubes

Slice the top off the Camembert and carefully scrape out the cheese, being careful not to pierce the rind. This operation is possible only if the cheese is well ripened. Set the rind aside.

Make a butter caramel by melting the sugar in a heavy-bottomed saucepan, adding the butter and cream away from the heat when the sugar has carmelized to a golden-brown. If the mixture sticks a bit, reheat it very gently and it will soften.

Blend the apples, cheese, and caramel together and fill the Camembert rind with the mixture. Serve warm or cold with good hazelnut or walnut bread.

Tip • It doesn't take a Nobel Prize for Physics to work out that not everything will fit back inside the empty Camembert rind once you've mixed the caramel and apples with the cheese. You will also realize that it's best to try out the recipes before inflicting them on your guests. Therefore…

Strawberries, red currants, and raspberries with raspberry sauce

This recipe depends upon the luck of the draw at your local grocery store or nearest farmer's market. Blackberries and blueberries are hard to find, but they would go very well in this pretty fruit salad.

Serves 6
Preparation time: 20 minutes
Cooking time: 5 minutes

2 cups strawberries, washed, hulled, and sliced
1 cup red currants, stripped and trimmed
2 cups raspberries
2 to 3 tbsp sugar

Mix the strawberries and red currants with half the raspberries. Put the remaining raspberries and the sugar in a saucepan, and cook gently for several minutes to make a purée. Strain this if you want to remove the raspberry seeds. Set aside to cool.

Just before serving, pour the purée over the other fruit and stir in.

Serve with vanilla-flavored mascarpone cheese, brandy snaps, or other crunchy little cookies and, perhaps, red-fruit sorbets.

Papaya and mango salad with orange juice and coconut snowballs

If you can't find coconut balls in the candie store or at an Asian market and, you haven't time to make your own, just sprinkle over some dried or flaked coconut instead.

Serves 6
Preparation time: 25 minutes

2 ripe papayas
3 ripe mangoes
Juice of 3 oranges
2 to 3 passion fruits (optional)
12 little coconut balls

Peel the papayas and mangoes, and cut the flesh into small dice. This is a bit fussy but gives a very pretty effect. If you simply do not have the time, cut the fruits into long strips.

Mix with the orange juice. If available, add the juice and seeds of 2 or 3 passion fruit to the orange juice.

Chocolate cookie cake

Serves 10
Preparation time: 25 minutes
Chilling time: overnight

6 tbsp butter, softened (I really like salted butter for
this cake, but suit yourself)
1⅓ cups icing sugar
3 tbsp cocoa powder blended in a little water
2 small packages very dark chocolate-topped cookies
2 to 3 coffee-cupfuls very strong black coffee

Blend the butter, icing sugar, and cocoa powder.

Soak the underside of each biscuit in the coffee for a few seconds
and arrange in a serving dish, making sure the cookies are pressed up
close to one another. Carefully spread a layer of butter–cream over.
Repeat the operation and top with a final layer of cookies.

Leave chilling in the refrigerator overnight if possible.

Triple choc-chip tartlets

Note: a flexible mold is essential for this dish. You can find these in catering specialists, kitchen shops, and sometimes in large department stores – mail order, too.

2 small packages Triple Choc-Chip cookies
5 tbsp salted butter
1 cup heavy cream
1 cup very dark chocolate (70% chocolate solids), broken into small pieces

Put the cookies in a large bowl and crush finely. Melt the butter and stir it into the cookies. Press the mixture into the cups of a flexible tart-mold, about 3 inches in diameter. Chill in the refrigerator.

Bring the cream to just boiling point and pour over the broken chocolate. Stir until it takes on a creamy, shiny consistency. Pour over the chilled cookie mixture and return to the refrigerator for several hours, until the chocolate cream firms up.

Unmold and serve.

Index

Recipe index

Drinks

Finger foods & mini sandwiches

Dips and sauces

Soups

Salads

Side dishes

Main dishes

Cheeses

Desserts

For Sophie and Nicolas, remember 2000

Acknowledgments

Thanks to: the tough nut, for the evening of flying saucers; Catherine and Florence for their valuable input; and Veronique, for the sweets. Amazing, there are some left! To Jacqueline, dinette-queen; La maison Ladurée for the magnificent showpiece on p. 7; and Eddie Barclay—nobody does it better.

And above all, to Thierry, Coco, Tim, Tanguy, and Victoire. Look, I'm here!

Shopping and art for the table: Pauline Ricard-André

Cardboard plates:
Tutti Fiesta – p.12, p.17, p.27.

Tableware:
Le Bon Marché Rive Gauche – p.45 (knife), p.83, p.125, p.127, p.179.
Léonardo – p.102.
Siècle – p.179 (mouse)
Tsé-Tsé – p.110, p.119.
Tutti Fiesta – p. 97 (plastic cutlery)

Plates and dishes:
Asa – p.120, p.129 (green plates), p.129, p.131, p.137, p.142, p.144.
Astier de Villatte – p.73 (dishes), p.76 (plates), p.79, pp.80 and 81 (plates), p.87, p.92, p.177 (fantasy plate).
Le Bon Marché Rive Gauche – p.18, p.49, p.58 (salad bowl), p.61 (bowl), p.107, p.135, p.159, p.169 (plates), p.173, p.177, p.179 (plate, bottom left), p.185.
Haviland – p.35 (by Franÿoise Bauchet), p.42, p.129, p.131.
Luneville – p.85.
Tsé-Tsé – p.55 (gratin dish), p.89, p.91, p.110, p.139 (shallow bowls), p.140 (plate).

Bowls and serving-dishes:
Asa – p.115 (square dish).
Astier de Villate – p.81.
Le Bon Marché Rive Gauche – p.49, p.83, p.107.
Haviland – p.39, p.51, p.119, p.123.
Léonardo – p.84, p.93.
Tsé-Tsé – p.22, p.23, p.25, p.27 (bowl).

Cloths, napkins, tablemats, tartans:
Cath Kidston – p.37, p.41, p.42, p.45, p.47, p.48.
Séquana – p.34

Glassware:
Le Bon Marché Rive Gauche – p.133, p.177.
Léonardo – p.57 (bowl), p.97 (glass).
Séquana – p.183.

Trays:
Tsé-Tsé – p.66, p.121, p.127.

This edition published by Silverback Books, Inc., San Francisco, California. www.silverbackbooks.com

French Team – Proofreaders and copyeditors: Véronique Dussidour and Antoine Pinchot; Shopping and Table Decoration: Pauline Ricard-André
North American Team – Production: Patty Holden; Food Editor: Ann Beman; Project Editor: Lisa M. Tooker
North American Version © 2004 Silverback Books, Inc.

Translation supplied by: ((PUBLISHER NEEDS TO ADD))

ISBN: 1-930603-83-5
Registration of copyright: ((PUBLISHER NEES TO ADD))

Printed in Sinapore by Tien Wah Press